Block, Marilyn R.

HQ
1059.5   Women over forty
.U5
B56

Springer Series

FOCUS ON WOMEN

Violet Franks, Ph.D., Series Editor

Confronting the major psychological, medical, and social issues of today and tomorrow, *Focus on Women* provides a wide range of books on the changing concerns of women.

VOLUME 1

THE SAFETY OF FERTILITY CONTROL

Editor-in-Chief: Louis G. Keith, M.D.
Associate Editors: Deryck R. Kent, M.D., Gary S. Berger, M.D., and Janelle R. Brittain, M.B.A.
With contributors

VOLUME 2

THERAPY WITH WOMEN
A Feminist Philosophy of Treatment

Susan Sturdivant, Ph.D.

VOLUME 3

SHELTERING BATTERED WOMEN
A National Study and Service Guide

Albert R. Roberts, D.S.W.

VOLUME 4

WOMEN OVER FORTY
Visions and Realities

Marilyn R. Block, Ph.D., Janice L. Davidson, M.S., and Jean D. Grambs, Ed.D.

MARILYN R. BLOCK, who received her Ph.D. in
Human Development from the University of Maryland, directs research projects for the Center on Aging
at the University of Maryland. She developed and still
teaches the first course on women and the aging process. She has a strong background in all aspects of
gerontology with special interests in the female aging
process and victimization of the elderly.

JANICE DAVIDSON, a Ph.D. candidate in Adult
Education at the University of Maryland, is a research
associate with the Center on Aging at the University of
Maryland. Her experiences focus on the areas of adult
education and development, gerontology, and women's
studies.

JEAN DRESDEN GRAMBS, who received her
Ed.D. in Educational Sociology from Stanford University, is a professor in the Human Development Department at the University of Maryland. She has extensive experience in all levels of education, with special emphasis in sex roles, women's issues, and aging.

Women Over Forty
Visions and Realities

Marilyn R. Block, Ph.D.
Janice L. Davidson, M.S.
Jean D. Grambs, Ed.D.

SPRINGER PUBLISHING COMPANY
New York

Springer Publishing Company, Inc.
200 Park Avenue South
New York, New York   10003

81 82 83 84 85 / 10 9 8 7 6 5 4 3 2 1

Library of Congress Cataloging in Publication Data

Block, Marilyn R.
  Women over forty.

  (Springer series, focus on women; 4)
  Bibliography: p.
  Includes index.
  1. Middle aged women—United States. I. Davidson, Janice L., joint author. II. Grambs, Jean Dresden, 1919–   joint author. III. Title. IV. Series.
HQ1059.5.U5B56   305.2'4   80-20774
ISBN 0-8261-3000-3
ISBN 0-8261-3001-1 (pbk.)

Printed in the United States of America

■
Contents

■ 6

■ 7

■
Preface

Any book that deals with psychologically significant and personally meaningful data presents special problems and opportunities for the authors. This volume is devoted to a factual presentation of the research about older women, so that myths and stereotypes will be challenged at every turn. Like other taboo areas in our culture, there is much negative imagery and unpleasant misinformation that may work destructively on the self-esteem of millions of individuals. Correct information about the normal extension of human development into mature adulthood and old age is the best preparation for these stages of life.

Although this book is intended primarily for students in gerontology, human development, and women's studies courses, the material is designed to be incorporated into related courses whose major focus is on some general aspect of social or psychological understanding. A course designed to examine the changing American family, for example, would find the material on the family status of older women (Chapter 6) useful.

Because of the previous failure of gerontologists, sociologists, psychologists, and policymakers to pay adequate attention to the older woman, this is an area in which advocacy is not only needed but inevitable. One way in which the academic community can assist in vital ways to meet the pressing needs of older women is to be sure that courses on the older woman are offered, or that relevant material on the older woman is incorporated as a matter of course in all gerontology, human development, and women's studies courses, and all other courses where such material has been traditionally omitted or overlooked. One important outcome of this kind of academic emphasis on the older woman should be increased research on the middle-aged and older woman. Other outcomes may well be more adequate services for older woman and policies that more nearly meet the particular needs of women growing older in our culture.

The project from which this book evolved was supported by Grant No. 90-A-1175(01) from the Administration on Aging, Department of Health and Human Services (formerly Department of Health, Education and Welfare). The findings, opinions, and conclusions expressed in this book, however, are solely those of the authors and do not necessarily reflect, nor can be inferred as being, the official position or policy of the Department of Health and Human Services.

Work on this book would not have been possible without the emotional support and practical suggestions provided by our families, friends, students, and colleagues. We especially appreciate the time devoted to this project by representatives of numerous aging and women's groups and organizations. A very special thank you must be offered to Priscilla M. Krisman, without whom the final manuscript would not have found its way to New York.

We hope to offer, through this book, support to the millions of wives, mothers, daughters, and sisters who are dealing with their own aging process each day of their lives.

Marilyn R. Block
Janice L. Davidson
Jean D. Grambs
College Park, Maryland

Introduction

Older women are here to stay. In fact, there are, and will be, more of them each succeeding decade. However, the literature on women has singularly failed to focus on the unique life experiences of the woman over 40. Literature in gerontology has been equally remiss in failing to examine the problems of older women as distinct from those encountered by aging men. Traditional approaches to gerontology have examined primarily those issues of aging pertinent to men while neglecting the issues specific to women. Yet because of their increased longevity, most older people are women. There are more than 12.8 million women in the United States aged 65 or older, and an additional 22 million women in the middle-aged population (ages 45–64). Together, these women comprise 16 percent of this country's inhabitants.

For too long these women have been "invisible." In addition to suffering the prejudices of ageism, older women are also subject to the prejudices of sexism. They occupy a difficult and unique position in our culture, partly as a result of their social isolation and relative longevity, partly as a result of their traditionally dependent status, and partly as a result of the inadequacies in our legislative and social systems in providing ample support to insure adequate living standards for our elderly population.

Older women in America today constitute the single poorest group of people in our society. For those women who have worked, this is due in large part to fewer years in the labor market at lower salaried jobs than men, resulting in lower social security and retirement benefits. It is partially due to the reluctance of employers to hire older women because of stereotyped attitudes that they are not adaptable to today's jobs and technology. And, finally, it is due somewhat to programs and agencies, such as the Social Security Administration, which to date have determined financial eligibility requirements according to traditional male standards, and so are unable to provide for the earlier and lengthier needs of women.

While life expectancy rates continue to climb for members of both sexes, women continue to benefit more than men from the declining death rate of the past fifty years. In 1975 the Census Bureau estimated that women would outlive their male counterparts by eight years, with life expectancy rates of 77 and 69, respectively. These figures have recently been revised upward. Life expectancy rates for men and women are now predicted at 72 and 81 respectively, for those born in 1978. But while both sexes are living longer, women will outlive men by *nine* years by the year 2050, instead of the eight years estimated in 1975.

That women benefit more than men from lessening mortality rates is further emphasized by the fact that, between 1960 and 1970, the population of women 65 and over increased twice as fast as the population of men 65 and over. In 1930, there were 1,006 men aged 65+ for every 1,000 women aged 65+; by 1970, this had declined to 722 men 65+ for every 1,000 women 65+.

Because women have longer life spans than men, and because women tend to marry older men, most women will experience widowhood. There are nearly six times as many widows as widowers. As one would expect, increasing age is accompanied by an increase in widowhood, so that by age 85, the proportion of women in a widowed state has reached 77 percent.

The high incidence of widowhood, an increasing divorce rate, and the numbers of women who never marry are all factors that contribute to loneliness and isolation. These are very real problems faced every day by middle-aged and older women. Because a man is still perceived by many as essential to a woman's worth, single older women (and single includes the widowed, divorced, and separated) are not viewed as having much to offer. Widows particularly are seldom invited to mixed social gatherings. A single woman does not "fit" in a couples-oriented world.

The American older woman also suffers from the double standard applied to the aging population. Males are viewed as increasingly attractive as they age, until fairly late in life. A touch of gray at the temples is considered distinguished. We do not find it at all impossible to imagine a Jacqueline Bisset attracted to a Cary Grant, but envisioning a Robert Redford falling for a Katherine Hepburn is difficult. The older woman is seen as asexual. She has lost her sex appeal as she has gained both years and experience. She is presumed to have neither the interest in nor the ability for a sexual relationship. Culturally, menopause marks the point in the older woman's life when she is washed up; she has lost her marketable attributes.

Such experiences should serve to draw older women together, to provide mutual support, for who can better understand the concerns of an older woman than another older woman who has shared many of the same experiences. Yet women helping women is a relatively untried concept for older age groups. This may be due in part to a socialization process that taught women to view other members of their sex as competition rather than as companions, confidantes, friends.

The problems of older women are severe, their resources limited. Their needs are many, yet these needs have not been explored in depth. A strong focus on childrearing and homemaking, coupled with the belief that they will be taken care of by the "system," leave many women ill-prepared to cope with their changing social roles at menopause, child-launching, and widowhood. This erosion of role-identity presents problems specific to women, problems that aging men will never experience.

The aging process can be difficult for a woman because of the loss of meaningful roles. Her children leave home, her husband often dies, and if she has not worked for a good part of her adult years, she has little preparation or skill for developing new productive roles to fill the gap. Too often she is left alone, discouraged, and without financial and emotional support. This is not only needlessly sad, but a waste of a valuable human resource. Strides have been made, but there is still much to do if we are to adequately meet the needs of the majority of the aging American population.

LACK OF DATA

Despite their greater numbers, women have not been the focus of most major research efforts in gerontology. The majority of researchers in gerontology have been, and are, male, and so tend to focus on the aging process of males. Additionally, subjects for studies have often been obtained from predominantly male populations, such as Veterans' Hospitals. Some researchers have deliberately excluded women from research studies because of the misconception that monthly hormonal changes would cause women to be unreliable subjects and bias test results.

WHAT IS "OLDER?"

The problems of definition and semantics arise when attempting a presentation of issues and concerns relevant to older women. For some, "older" is chronologically defined: On reaching a particular age, one's status is somehow altered. For others, the concept of "you're as old as you feel" applies: One is not "older" until one perceives certain physical and attitudinal changes.

For the purposes of this book, "older" has been defined in terms of major life events or milestones. A number of physiological and social changes occur during the decade of the 40s that determine, for many women, the direction of the aging process. Thus, the socially defined age of 65 as "older" has no relevance to this undertaking, since the milestones of the preceding 20 years are not accounted for. Therefore, our "older" woman is not an *old* woman; she is also middle-aged. For the chronologically oriented, the older woman is approximately 45 years of age and older.

OVERVIEW OF CHAPTERS

The first chapter in the book, "A Demographic Profile of the Older Woman in America," reveals important twentieth-century trends that have strongly influenced the status of women. Specific topics include population distribution, geographic distribution, life expectancy, marital status, living arrangements, education, employment, and income with regard to older women.

Chapter 2, "Images of Older Women," examines the ways in which older women are perceived in American society, how these perceptions have developed, and what effects myths and stereotypes have had on the self-image of older women. It also examines the socialization process of women and lays the foundation for the chapters that follow.

Chapters 3 and 4 focus on a variety of health issues of special concern to older women. Chapter 3, "Menopause and Sexuality," examines the physiological process of menopause and explores the question of estrogen-replacement therapy. The double standard of male and female sexuality is also questioned. Chapter 3 also presents available data on three medical conditions frequently encountered by middle-aged and older women: hysterectomy, osteoporosis, and breast cancer. The issues of stress, depression, suicide, drug abuse, and alcoholism are discussed in Chapter 4, "Mental Health and Related Issues."

The fifth chapter, "Life Situations," describes how role changes, social interactions, friendship patterns, and living arrangements may have positive or negative impact upon women's life styles. Chapter 6, "Family Relations," probes the factors that may cause changes in a woman's relationships with various members of her family, such as children leaving home, retirement, divorce, widowhood, being a grandmother, and relationships between adult children and aging parents.

Chapter 7, "Employment and Retirement," takes a more pragmatic turn. The antecedents of work aspiration and choice, as well as available opportunities for work are explored. The subsection on continuing education clarifies the concept of returning, or reentry, women and discusses the personal and occupational implications of this relatively recent educational phenomenon. Emotional adjustment to retirement is examined, as is the economic impact of retirement vis-à-vis social security and pension benefits available to women.

Most research done in the United States on older women has used white women as subjects. Because 85 percent of women at all ages, and 90 percent of women over 45, are white, this research is valid. But equally important is the aging process of other groups of women. Chapter 8, "Ethnic and Racial Variations in Older Women," explores the significance of being an older woman who belongs to a minority group such as Hispanic, Jewish, American Indian, Asian American, or black.

While each chapter is as complete as the available literature will allow, we acknowledge the need for additional research in these and many more areas, in order to fill in the many gaps that currently exist. Thus, Chapter 9, "Research Issues," presents a variety of questions and concerns that have received little, if any, serious attention from researchers in the field of gerontology.

■ 1
A Demographic Profile of the Older Woman in America

This chapter highlights information concerning the impact of changing social and economic conditions. Demographic data on older women reveal some important trends that significantly affect their status. In examining the statistical information on specific issues concerning the older woman as provided by various sources across time, we see that numbers alone are not significant unless they can be interpreted with some meaning in terms of cause and effect. Why have these numbers changed and in what ways will they have an effect on the future of older women in the United States?

It is necessary to understand the concept of cohort if demographic trends are to be accurately interpreted. As used in demography, *cohort* refers to those individuals born within a certain time span, usually a specified period, either 1 year, or 5 years, or 10, and subject, as a result, to specific social and historical pressures and events that may be unique. Cohort effect is particularly important in comparing women of the same age at different points in time. The woman of 50 in 1960 (cohort 1910) may have a very different set of values and expectations in comparison to the woman who will be 50 in 1990 (cohort 1940).

The data, as they appear in current statistical reports, focus on the following topics with regard to older women: population distribution;

geographic distribution; life expectancy; marital status; living arrangements; education; employment; and income.

POPULATION DISTRIBUTION

Because of their increased longevity, most older people in the United States today are women. In 1900 approximately 50 percent of the elderly population were women. By 1977 this figure had risen to 59 percent. As of July 1977 13.7 million women in the United States were aged 65 or older, and an additional 22 million women were middle-aged (45–64 years). Together these women comprised 16 percent of this country's inhabitants.

Since 1900 older women have consistently become a larger proportion of the *female* population. Between 1960 and 1974 the number of older women increased 42 percent as compared to 18 percent for the total population and 32 percent for the older population. Projections for the year 2000 indicate that although the number of older women will continue to increase, the distribution among separate age groups will decrease for the 65–69-year-olds, remain stable for the 70–74-year-olds, and increase for those in the over-75 age groups. These shifts in the distributions reflect the fact that women are living longer, and an increasing number of women will live beyond the age of 75.

An examination of the racial composition of the older female population points to an increase in elderly minority women that in no way compares to the proportional gains in life span made by older white women. Only 7.7 percent of the black population in 1974 was comprised of women over the age of 65, whereas older white women accounted for 11.9 percent of the white population. These large differences have been due, in part, to the higher fertility of the black population (causing larger percentages of young blacks in the total black population), a lower rate of mortality among young blacks (resulting in greater numbers of blacks at younger ages), and to the large number of adult nonblack immigrants before World War I.

Blacks, however, fare much better than older women of Hispanic origin (Mexican-American, Puerto Rican, Cuban, and South American). In 1974 only 3.8 percent of the female population of Hispanic origin were over 65 years old (U.S. Dept. of Commerce, 1976a). This low percentage is due in part to many of the same factors affecting the black population. In addition, more males than females were among the immigrants of Hispanic descent.

Among the 13.2 million elderly women in the United States in 1975, 91 percent were white, 7 percent were black, and approximately 2 percent were of Hispanic origin. Other minority ethnic groups, such as Asian and native Americans, made up less than 1 percent of the total female population aged 65 and over.

As the number of older women in the United States increases, so too does the ratio of older women to older men. Compared to the 13.7 million older women in 1977, there were 9.4 million older men. Projections for the year 2000 reveal a 34.9 percent increase to 18.6 million older women, compared to 12 million men, indicating a still larger sex ratio. The large proportion of older women to older men has been the most noticeable change to occur for these age groups within the past 75 years, and is directly related to the widening gap between the male and female rate of mortality.

GEOGRAPHIC DISTRIBUTION

The residential and migratory patterns of the older woman are influenced by a variety of factors, including health, income, marital status, and age. Age, however, does not appear to be a determinant of whether a woman lives in an urban or a rural setting. According to the 1970 census, over 70 percent of women at *every* age level were living in urban areas, especially in central cities. Very few older women settled in suburban environments. Although reasons for this are not given, it is probable that income and transportation problems prevent the older woman from living in the suburbs. (Of the women over 65 living in rural areas, the majority are not on farms but in small towns.) A similar distribution is true for males over 65, with one notable exception: a much larger percentage of males live in rural farm settings (U.S. Dept. of Commerce, 1976a).

As one might expect, almost half of the elderly women live in seven of the eight most populous states. Of these states, California and New York have more than one million older women each, with Florida, Illinois, Ohio, Pennsylvania, and Texas claiming at least one-half million apiece. The geographic pattern of older men is not significantly different. More than likely these states will continue to have large numbers of elderly women, because most older women remain where they are. When older women do move, however, they usually go to a place designed for retirement, settle in a small town, move in with relatives, or return to their country of origin (U.S. Dept. of Commerce, 1976a).

LIFE EXPECTANCY

The years that remain in a person's life on reaching a certain age are referred to as one's life expectancy. Older women have a longer life expectancy than older men.

Life expectancy rates can be very deceptive since they account for several subtle variables. First, they reflect infant and child mortality rates that, when taken into account, effectively lower life expectancy. Once an individual lives to age 65 he or she will tend to live longer than the average life expectancy because the possibility of childhood death has been bypassed. Those males who live to age 65 should live another 13 years to age 78. Those females who live to age 65 should live another 18 years to age 83. (Sixty-seven percent of all males and 81 percent of all females live to age 65.)

Second, life expectancy rates must account for cohort effect. Because each generation is exposed to advances in prenatal care, improved childbirth practices, and mass immunizations, as well as increased knowledge about nutrition and hygiene, successive generations can expect longer life spans. A baby girl born in 1900 could expect to live to age 48, while a baby girl born in 1977 can anticipate an 81-year life span.

Although the mortality rate for both males and females is decreasing, in 1974 the rate for men was 90 percent higher than for women. If the death rates remain the same, 81 percent of female as opposed to 67 percent of male children will live to be 65. Males appear to have a higher death rate almost from the beginning. Despite the fact that more male babies are born than females, the numbers tend to even out by the time they reach their twenties. Infant mortality is greater for males than for females because males have more genetic defects and are more vulnerable to disease.

Factors affecting the woman's longevity might be traced back to the environment or to individual heredity. Despite the changing roles of men and women, men more frequently achieve positions that are physically and mentally demanding. Additionally, they are more frequently victims of accidents and homicide. It has often been noted that women seem to have a better or stronger capacity for survival. For the most part, however, the life expectancy for the woman has been enhanced by the reduction of deaths caused by difficulties during childbirth and pregnancy and the legalization of abortion. In addition, diseases causing death among the elderly, such as heart disease and cancer caused by smoking, affect men more than women.

The mortality rates for males and females are quite distinct for all races, but especially so for white males and females. Although the life expectancy for older women of different racial and ethnic groups at age 65 is greater in comparison to the men of these groups, older white women still live longer than older women of other backgrounds. In 1973 white women at age 65 could expect to live 1.1 years longer than black women of the same age. This is a remarkably small difference, considering that the average life expectancy for blacks has almost doubled since 1900. The increase in average life expectancy for blacks is a result of the decrease in immigration, the reduction of white childbirths, and the improved health conditions of blacks.

Health problems are a major concern to the elderly population regardless of race. It is also a costly concern, because three times more money is spent on health care for the elderly than for young persons (Kimmel, 1974). Very little demographic data are available on the older woman and her health, but what is known is not particularly heartening. Older women may live longer than men, but they also have a greater chance of acquiring some kind of disability that will limit their activities to a great degree for a long period of time. Eighty-five percent of women over 65 have some kind of chronic health problem. The incidence of heart disease is twice as high for men as for women between ages of 65 and 74, and cancer is also more likely to occur in older men than women, but these two diseases are also the leading causes of death in the elderly female population (Kimmel, 1974; U.S. Dept. of Commerce, 1976a).

MARITAL STATUS

In 1970 31 percent of 25-year-old women who married 30-year-old men could expect to be widows before the husbands reached age 65, and 42 percent would be widowed after the husband passed the 65-year-old mark. By 1975, of the men over 65 years of age, 77 percent were married compared to 52 percent of the women who were widows. In 1976 an estimated 7.2 million women over 65 were widows, nearly 1 million were single, and 3.9 million were married. By the age of 60, 20 percent of American women are widows; by 65, the average is 50 percent; and by 75, almost 68 percent are widows. In 1977 there were 5 times as many widows as widowers.

Projections for the year 2000 show a decrease in the percentage of women over 65 who have never married, while *at the same time indicating that a much larger proportion of older women will be divorced*. A 10 percent increase, from 12 percent to 22 percent, is expected between 1975 and 2000 in the number of women being divorced (Glick, 1977). The numbers of single elderly women will undoubtedly increase as a result. The older woman has few chances of getting married. More than one-third of the eligible older men will marry younger women, and most elderly men are already married. Three out of four elderly men over age 65 are married as compared to one out of three women (Troll, 1971).

There are several explanations to account for the low number of married elderly women. The higher mortality rate for older men coupled with the fact that most men marry younger than themselves results in more widows than widowers. While it has long been socially acceptable for older men to marry younger women, there exists a strong taboo against older women marrying younger men.

LIVING ARRANGEMENTS

Of women over 65 years of age in 1975, 59 percent were members of families: 36 percent had husbands as head of households and 23 percent resided with family members other than a husband. An estimated 36 percent of women over 65 were living alone, while for men the figure was closer to 14 percent. Projections for 1984 indicate an increase (to 43 percent) in the number of women living alone. Only a small proportion of older women (5 percent) are institutionalized at any given time, although estimates indicate that 20 percent of all older women will live in an institution at some point.

EDUCATION

As there are changes in the quantity of older women, so also are there changes in the quality of life for older women. The rate of illiteracy among the older population will consistently decrease as new cohorts of more educated members move into the ranks of the older age groups.

In 1974 more than 66 percent of the women aged 25–64 had at least a high school education and 11 percent had completed college. These figures are less for women over 65: 33 percent had finished high school and 6 percent college. The median number of school years for women who will be over 65 in 2000 is projected to be 12.1 in comparison to the 9.4 years attained by the older woman of 1975. The continuing education movement is, in large part, responsible for this change. More and more older women are opting to complete the educaton that had been pushed aside for home and family duties. Universities and colleges are avidly pursuing them, too, as a new student market to compensate for enrollment declines.

EMPLOYMENT

Changes have occurred for the older woman in terms of her participation in the labor force. More and more older women are looking for work, often out of necessity. Despite the fact that only 1 out of 13 older women (compared to 1 out of 5 older men) was job hunting in 1976, the middle-aged and older woman's participation in the labor force has doubled since 1954. In 1960 the rates leveled off; recent reports indicate that these rates are remaining fairly steady. In 1976 between 8–10 percent of the population of women over 65 were employed, whereas over 20 percent of comparably aged men were in the labor force. In that same year, nearly half (48 percent) of all middle-aged women (ages 45–64) were employed, as compared to almost 90 percent of similarly aged males (U.S. Dept. of Commerce, 1977b).

The amount of education older women have acquired is correlated with the amount of time these women will work. For women between the ages of 30 and 44, having at least 1 year of college, 21 percent have worked an average of 6 months out of every year since leaving school. Women in the same age group having completed college will work an average of 8 months out of every year since leaving school. These data suggest that women with a higher level of education will probably work more than those with less schooling, and in turn will probably earn more in wages. Unfortunately, the woman currently between the ages of 45 and 54 has, on the average, only been working about half the number of years as the average man in the same age group. Thus, she will have less income, less opportunity to see her earnings reach their potential peak, and she will receive significantly less on retirement.

INCOME

If a person is a female over the age of 65 in the 1970s she will have more than a 50 percent chance of being poor. Women constitute 65 percent of the elderly who are poor. The elderly person is expected to survive on less than half of what a young person receives as income. Women over 65 had the smallest income of all women over the age of 35 who were employed.

There also appears to be some relationship between the older woman's living arrangements and her income. In 1974 older women living alone had lower incomes than women who were heads of families. About 33 percent of women who lived alone were below the poverty level, while only 13 percent of families headed by older women fell into this category. Over half of the families with women as heads brought in less than $7,723, and 10 percent made less than $3,000; 19 percent received between $10,000 and $15,000; and 18 percent got over $15,000.

SUMMARY

Despite the problems that constantly confront them, women appear to have a superior vitality that enables them to live more years than most men. The number of older women has increased dramatically since the turn of the century as compared to the older population in general. Life expectancy is influenced to a large degree by cohort. The majority of women live to age 65; those who live to age 65 can anticipate a life span of 83 years; but 85 percent of women over 65 can anticipate some kind of chronic health problem.

But this longevity is a mixed blessing, since older women in 1978 are poorer, less educated, less employed, and more alone than older men.

Older women are among the poorest groups of individuals in the United States, the majority of whom live in urban areas, and nearly half of whom live in seven of the eight most populous states. Women over the age of 65 have better than a 50 percent chance of being poor.

Despite rapidly growing continuing education programs, few older women complete college. The median number of school years for women over the age of 65 is projected to increase from 9.4 in 1975 to 12.1 in 2000. Nearly half of all middle-aged women were employed in 1976. As the woman's level of education increases, so does the likelihood that she will seek work.

There are 5 times as many widows as widowers. Half of American women are widowed by age 65, and by age 75 the incidence has increased to 68 percent. An equal number of older women live either alone or with a spouse. Of the remaining percentage of women over 65, most live with other family members. Only a small percentage of older women are institutionalized at any one time.

The demographic realities of the plight of older women are becoming an increasingly acute problem, to the extent that the Select Committee on Population has focused special hearings on the needs of this group. A greater understanding of demographic changes and their future impact on women is critical. As these economic, educational, and employment inequities are understood and rectified, a less dismal picture will be painted for future cohorts.

■2
Images of Older Women

Older women are in a double bind: we are expected to feel inferior not only as women, but also because we are too old (Janeway, 1973).

In this chapter, an attempt will be made to examine how older women are perceived in American society, how these perceptions have developed, and whether they accord with the facts. So many generalizations have been made about older women that in today's society myths and stereotypes abound. Until recently, a lack of interest in older women prevented the facts from being known. Even though the realities are now becoming better known, the negative and stereotypic attitudes toward older women that are held by the vast majority of the American people are slow to change.

While it is unrealistic to assume that all older women are alike, it is also unrealistic to assume that older women have nothing in common. In exploring these similarities and differences, therefore, it is important to keep in mind the uniqueness of these women as individuals. For example, the term "older women" employed herein at no time refers to *all* older women.

What then are these myths and stereotypes? What effects have they had on older women? What are the realities about older women and what is being done to make then known? The answers to these questions are

11

important to every female: those who are old and those who will one day be old.

MYTHS AND STEREOTYPES

The image of the older woman as an inactive, unhealthy, asexual, and ineffective person has been perpetuated over the years through the transmission of inaccurate information. The cultural denigration of older women is taught through fairy tales and children's picture books. Adult magazines and television programming foster these attitudes through adolescence and young adulthood. Regardless of what profession or status a woman holds, she still sees aging as a negative aspect of her life. This stems in large part from the negative reception she encounters in the outside world.

After looking at the facts available on the older woman as presented in various research reports and scholarly journals, Payne and Whittington (1976) tried to "demythologize" the older woman in American society. They have indicated that the three major components of an older woman's life around which the stereotypes center are health, marital status, and leisure activities. Authorities differ on the source of the myths or which of the stereotypes are most widely believed, but they generally agree on the nature of the stereotypes.

For the most part, treatment of the older woman's image has been rather negative. Older women have been ridiculed in numerous jokes; they have been depicted as old maids, making awkward (and usually unsuccessful) efforts to conceal their age. In essence, these attempts at humor reflect social attitudes toward the aging woman (Palmore, 1971). According to Livson (1977), these negative perceptions of older women have been a part of history, carried down through time ever since early religions' beliefs incorporated a fear and envy of the mother goddess. She relates this concept to man's dependence on his own mother goddess, which produced a resentment so deep that there exists within him a lasting drive to "establish dominance over woman politically and sexually—to devalue her status and deny the power he projects onto her" (Livson, 1977, p. 3).

Older women have long been regarded as sexless creatures who lack the desire or the potential to engage in sexual activities. Yet research shows that age does not hinder the older woman's sexual capacity. It brings with it, however, the probability that the older woman will have a smaller opportunity to find an available male sex partner, for younger men seldom approach women who are much older, and older men usually prefer young women. With over half of the older women in the United States widowed, it is possible that many of them are inactive sexually because they lack a male partner, *not* because they lack the interest. Perhaps if aging in women were more socially acceptable, the older woman would not be perceived as excluded from leading a normal sex life.

In matters of health, older women have been regarded as less healthy than older men (Riley and Foner, 1968), even though they outlive men by some seven years. The image of the older woman as a hypochondriac is another myth that is held by many, but is not supported in the literature. A longitudinal investigation by Duke University produced data that indicated no significant difference between the health of men and women as rated by themselves and physicians. Despite the myth that men are healthier than women, the fact remains that on the average women do live longer than men. This longevity has been attributed to the social and psychological variables of happiness, performance IQ, and socioeconomic status (Palmore and Manton, 1973). Other predictors of longevity have been found to be self-perception of health change, marital status, and how one functions physically (Pfeiffer, 1970). Older women may have an advantage over men in terms of life expectancy, but this is not so where their identity is concerned.

The prevailing image of the older woman is that of a dependent, passive person whose identification rests on her connection to a man, while a man is seen to have an identity that does not depend on a woman. Older women are finding it difficult to shake off the limitations that derive from this kind of identification with their husbands (Payne and Whittington, 1976). Women who have realized this type of psychological dependence and are widowed discover that they are not prepared for the independence that has been thrust on them (Kethley, 1975). Some of these widows are learning to enjoy their newly found freedom. They do not want to pursue the roles that society expected of them as wives. Instead, they are looking forward to new engagements in leisure time activities, volunteer work, or in paying occupations. Widowhood, however, brings with it more than independence for the older woman. The financial, social, and psychological problems with which older women are faced at this time can be overwhelming, especially for those women who become widows in the later years, never having lived alone before.

Poverty is not an uncommon phenomenon for older women. They

receive no benefits commensurate for the work they have performed as housewives. Even those who are employed receive less than employed men of the same age. For many, the new responsibility of handling the finances is an added burden. Trying to make ends meet and faced with the possibility of living for quite a few more years, older women must cope with a harsh future.

Older women must also contend with social and cultural isolation (Lewis and Butler, 1972). Although they do keep in contact with relatives, older women who are widows are distressed to discover that with the loss of their husbands they also lose friends. Alone, with few social acquaintances left, the older woman does not go out much. Many older women, fearing they will be victimized by thieves, muggers, and even rapists, do not venture far from home. Older women would undoubtedly enjoy getting out more, but circumstances have forced them into an unhappy isolation.

While social isolation usually affects widowed older women, cultural isolation is a common occurrence for older women in general. The absence of older women in various forms of the media underscores this isolation. For example, women over the age of sixty are noticeably lacking in American magazine fiction (Martel, 1968). Television is also guilty of keeping the older woman out of sight. Although older women outnumber older men in the real world, they are significantly fewer in number in the world of television (Northcott, 1975). Limited media exposure is further evidence of the lower status that women attain as they age, and the cultural belief that older women are not subjects of interest to a viewing audience.

Cultural isolation is also evident in the fact that old age in women can be a handicap for those who would like to improve their situation by returning to school or starting a new occupation. Recent studies suggest that older women make good students and reliable employees, but the outside world is not ready to accommodate them. Such negative attitudes and stereotypes act as barriers to women who want to make changes in their lives.

More often than not, however, the older woman is perceived as not interested in such "inappropriate" activities. The image of the older woman is more likely to be that of the kind little old granny who spends her days knitting in her rocking chair and attending church socials.

In addition to participating in religiously affiliated groups, older women frequently serve as volunteers in various organizations, particularly those that are charitable. Older women turn out to volunteer in greater numbers than older men, but they have a higher dropout rate. Perhaps this will change, because older women are beginning to realize that their roles as volunteers are valuable and instrumental (Payne, 1973).

Given how negatively older women are viewed by American society, one would expect them to have a multitude of psychological problems. The information available on this subject is conflicting. It is reported that women of middle-age suffer mental disorders three to four times as much as middle-aged men (Bell, 1970). As women age, it is said that they have a greater probability than men of having psychiatric difficulties. Many of the older woman's problems are thought to be directly linked to menopause. In fact, some doctors tend to treat the older woman's health problems, regardless of the symptoms, as a postmenopausal syndrome or as senility (Beeson, 1975). (Chapter Three explores the issue of menopause in detail.)

Some theorists argue over the effects of widowhood and retirement on the psychological status of the older woman. While role theorists claim that widows or women who retire undergo few problems in making the required adjustments, articles written by older women and studies of older women reveal that these periods in their lives are indeed emotionally stressful. Women's retirement brings with it the likelihood of significant psychological trauma. There is no evidence that women come out psychologically unscathed from the loss of a mate (Lowenthal, Berkman, and Associates, 1967).

Although the image of the older woman is generally rather negative, some studies indicate a more positive attitude toward older women. In one study comparing young and old men and women on potential performance, older women were rated as objectively as the young men on the basis of their performance (Walsh and Connor, 1977).

Older women are also believed to be envied for their ability to be independent. This independence is a cross-cultural phenomenon that is achieved by postmenopausal women (Safilios-Rothschild, 1977). In some countries, older women are free to walk unescorted, to interact with men, and to engage in some kind of business enterprise, privileges not accorded younger women. A number of cultures permit older women to exercise power and authority over all younger women in the extended family. As a result, younger women in these societies often eagerly anticipate the acquisition of privileges that accompanies middle and old age.

Until more research looks at the difference between older men and women, it will be impossible to separate the misconceptions from the reality of the older woman's existence. While there is some basis for the minority viewpoints expressed by people, most of the stereotypes and attitudes toward older women are negative. It is also becoming evident that these negative perceptions of older women are held not only by society but also by older women themselves.

SELF-IMAGE

If people would quit accenting age—I'd probably never realize I'm 51, but when I'm turned away from the YWCA because I'm too old. . . . I'd forgotten what the "Y" stood for in YWCA (Brown, 1973).

I don't have any fears and tragedies that I had when I was younger. I can say what I feel, I am not embarrassed by many things any more, and my personality is better (Lowenthal, Thurnher, and Chiriboga, 1975).

Think what it is . . . to be told every day that you are not a woman but a tired object that should disappear. . . . I am bitter and frustrated and wasted. . . . (Moss, 1970).

I really like people. I am the kind who gives a lot. . . . I have the nature that makes people lean on me (Clark and Anderson, 1967).

We're frightened of leaving the secure nest, the pale where we have things under control (Bergquist, 1973).

Just as there are different opinions about the way in which older women are perceived, so too are there differing points of view about the older woman's self-image. Sweeping generalizations about how older women see themselves should be avoided, for it is from just such statements that stereotypes and misconceptions are formed. The available information on the older woman's self-image needs to be reviewed carefully so that the accumulated evidence can be interpreted and discrepancies identified.

Older women do not have to accept society's perception of them. Instead, older women can have positive self-images that reflect their personal attitudes; those older women who have negative self-images in old age more than likely had negative self-images in their younger years (Clark and Anderson, 1967). This theory is further supported by a longitudinal study in which the personality of young parents was found to continue into old age (Maas and Kuypers, 1975). It must be noted, however, that older women encounter more discontinuities in life that can affect ego identity, resulting in some changes in personality.

It has been reported (Clark and Anderson, 1967) that older women have a more positive self-image than older men because they are more socially involved and have more friends. Self-report data indicate that in later life men and women differ slightly in their self-ratings; women become more positive about their image as they age (Lowenthal, Thurnher, and Chiriboga, 1975). Further, women in the preretirement stage are beginning to view themselves as less dependent, less helpless, less disorderly and self-indulgent, and as more assertive and effective.

Those who contend that older women have positive self-concepts rely on the lack of support of the women's movement by older women as further evidence. The implication is that if older women were dissatisfied with their lives, they would join the women's liberation movement and voice their objections. What is not considered, however, is the fact that it would be very difficult for older women to speak out against the very roles they performed for the greater part of their lives. By doing so, they would, in effect, be attacking the source of their own self-esteem. Avoidance of women's issues may be a necessary means of defense for older women, but it does not necessarily imply that older women have positive self-images (Janeway, 1973).

While some of the literature portrays a positive self-image of older women, a major portion provides evidence to the contrary. In one personal account older women are called "retreads" who, because of "isolation, socialization, or mind-set, think our shaky confidence, malaise, boredom, feelings of going-to-waste, guilt about wanting to do 'selfish' things on our own, are part of some private, personal hang-up" (Bergquist, 1973). This type of attitude in older women has been associated with the kind of identity crises that one finds in the autobiographical literature.

One identity crisis is said to begin with the "empty nest" syndrome, which occurs when the children have all moved away from home. Women who have devoted their lives to caring for their families find themselves facing new feelings of anxiety and depression with the loss of a major role (Higgins, 1975). Many women may not feel this way. One study pointed out that older women, relieved to be free of the responsibilities of raising a family, had more positive self-concepts (Lowenthal, Thurnher, and Chiriboga, 1975).

For women who have achieved their own identity through recognition of their accomplishments, the sense of role loss may not arrive until retirement. Even so, these older women may not have the high self-esteem that might be expected, because they feel that they are rejected by other women who may be envious or who may look down on a role that was not deemed feminine (Janeway, 1973). It is also possible that older women who are considering a reentry to the labor market will be going into it with a lack of confidence in their abilities, and will have their low self-image further diminished by employers who are reluctant to hire them or who place them in jobs far below their education or ability. If, however, these women are being encouraged to reenter the work force, their self-concepts will improve as they make more contacts, bring more money into the home, gain the respect of their husbands, and encourage self-reliance in their children (Bergquist, 1973).

There is little doubt, however, about the self-image of someone who makes the comment, "There is no prestige attached to having sex with me" (Moss, 1970, p. 174). Dependent on physical appearance and youth for part of their identity and self-worth, older women are forced to think less of themselves, because facial lines and wrinkled skin are devalued in American society. Positive feedback is important for self-esteem, but older women are least apt to receive any. Women are expected to not only look young and feminine, but to act feminine. Expecting older women to engage in more feminine roles, however, may be more damaging to the self-concept than would be imagined. It was discovered that preretirement women who endorsed the feminine role or rejected the masculine role ranked higher on self-criticism (Lowenthal, Thurnher, and Chiriboga, 1975). This might be one explanation for the decreasing differences between men's and women's self-concepts as they grow older, for older women are known to assume feminine interests but to exhibit masculine personality traits such as competitiveness and aggressiveness (Huyck, 1974).

Although older women have different self-images, these images derive from a common focus on the social roles of women. Understanding the process of socialization in women may shed some light on the importance of social roles as they relate to the self-images of older women.

SOCIALIZATION

By the time women have reached old age, they have experienced a series of roles that are both continuous and discontinuous (Prock, 1975). These roles are the result of a process of socialization through which women have learned to adapt to and carry out certain social expectations. It is also the process that determines which norms, standards, and values are transmitted from generation to generation (Neugarten and Datan, 1973).

The perception that they have not lived up to the expectations of society may cause some older women to undergo an identity crisis. In one study on femininity, the authors (Pishkin and Thorne, 1977) concluded that women face problems in relation to their roles as mothers and wives and also about their social roles. These problems are being revealed by the increasing number of women who are finding it difficult to cope with the pressures imposed on them by society and who are at odds with their own needs for personal fulfillment.

Today's older women have been socialized to the extent that they have learned to live with the traditional female role of passivity and subordination. Many older women have been socialized to accept their role as the force behind a man's success, but not to expect to do anything that will receive visible recognition. Today's 60-year-old was born in 1919, a 70-year-old in 1909. Expectations of sex role appropriate behavior were quite different during their formative years than for the women who are 20 or 30 today.

Kline (1975) suggests that "role inconstancy rather than constancy may account for feminine resilience in old age." Not only do roles change, but they also tend to overlap and conflict with each other. A great many women handle these role shifts successfully and as a result will better enjoy their old age.

The one role with which most older women can identify is that of mother. These women have grown up believing that they would not be complete without bearing children. They see it as a role that takes priority even over their roles as housewives. In the past motherhood left little room for much else, and so when it was time for the children to leave home, these older women were perplexed as to what to do with the extra time and how to fill the void made by the role loss.

The role of wife also changes with divorce or the death of the spouse. For women the role of spouse is rated more highly than for men (Zimmerman, 1974). For older women such as displaced homemakers and widows, social roles change radically with the loss of a mate. Being single in old age is in no way comparable to being single and young. Contemporary society does not plan for these older, single women.

Plans have not been made for the older women in the world of employment. Women who have worked for wages most of their lives are accommodated in the job market, but few employers want to bother with older women who have few or no skills. Many of today's older women hadn't anticipated having to work outside the home once they were married. They hadn't forseen the possibility that inflation would make them poverty-stricken in old age.

For older women, retirement implies more than just retiring from an occupation. As she grows older, a woman might retire several times. She might retire as a housewife, as a mother, or as an employee. Each retirement requires the woman to make adjustments, and it is proposed that these repeated adjustments to change facilitiate the adjustment in old age (Kline, 1975). Such impermanence in life roles was found to be a contributing factor to the life satisfaction of women between the ages of 50 and 60, thereby indicating that the socialization of women in later life can be just as influential as that in their younger years (Mulvey, 1973).

The retirement of older women from the work force is just as difficult as it is for older men. Differences in work orientation between older men and women are negligible, and women do regard work to be important for them, not only for financial reasons. In many cases, retiring older women exhibit the psychological symptoms of loneliness, anxiety, depression, and an unstable self-concept (Atchley, 1976).

The effects of retirement on older women are signals of a changing image of older women brought about by a change in the socialization of women. One source warns that women in industrial societies may attain equal status with men, but at the expense of becoming depersonalized (Murphy and Murphy, 1976).

Women are beginning to receive help through counseling and discussion sessions on various unexplored topics, such as the problems encountered in role changes. Older women in the future will have more models of women who have been recognized and honored for their achievements. The goal for these women will be self-actualization through many pathways. Older women will then be able to look back on their lives with satisfaction, knowing that they have accomplished their goals, whether they were raising a family, pursuing a career, participating in public life—or all of these. Women who never marry will not be pitied, and women who marry will be treated as an equal partner in the marriage.

SUMMARY

So that the images of older women, today and in the future, will be viewed more positively by older women and the rest of society, stereotypes must be challenged. Older women must be depicted more accurately, with diverse interests and life styles, expressing their individuality in different ways, and having, through their life experiences, valuable contributions to offer to willing recipients.

Older women are beginning to make their presence felt by joining forces in such organizations as the Gray Panthers and NOW and providing vigorous leadership. As people have contact with the increasing numbers of older women returning to the college campus and reentering the job market, more accurate perceptions of older women will be transmitted to the public. As older women, who kept, and were previously kept, out of the public eye, become more and more visible, the existing negative and stereotyped images of them will eventually disappear.

■3
Menopause and Sexuality

In a culture where sexual appeal and motherhood are considered the highest virtues, menopause for women often signals a figurative *"end* of life" rather than *"change* of life." In earlier centuries and other cultures, most women died before reaching menopause. Because menopause is a culturally new phenomenon, there exist no cultural norms and relatively little research data. Thus, America's youth-oriented culture results in both men and women viewing menopause as the inexorable descent of women into middle and old age. One common misconception is that menopause marks the end of sexual interest and activity. Because children are moving out of their parents' homes at about the onset of menopause, it also may be interpreted as the end of a woman's social role—childbearing and child-rearing. These cultural beliefs cannot help but have a heavy psychological impact on the woman experiencing this normal physical change. The purpose of this chapter is to examine the physical and psychological antecedents to, as well as the consequences of, menopause. The issues of sexuality and changing health status will also be addressed.

MENOPAUSE

According to Posner (1979), menopause continues to be poorly understood, perhaps "because menstruation can be seen as a positive sign of womanhood, of youth, of reproductive ability, while menopause remains a stigma, a symbol of decrepitude and decay" (p. 181). The popular image of the typical menopausal woman "is negative—she is exhausted, haggard, irritable, bitchy, unsexy, impossible to life with, driving her husband to seek other women's company, irrationally depressed, unwillingly suffering a 'change' that marks the end of her active (re)productive life" (Boston Women's Health Book Collective, 1976, p. 229).

This view of menopause as an affliction causes some women to avoid admitting they are menopausal. They fear going crazy, losing their husbands, and being relegated to the discard heap (Women's Medical Center, 1977). Unfortunately, members of the helping professions (such as doctors and psychotherapists) subscribe to the myth that menopause offers the probability of dangerous psychological crisis. Those women who do approach their doctors with problems are often tagged as neurotic and treated with tranquilizers (such as Valium) or with estrogen. In fact, many women aged 40+ who present physical or emotional problems are labeled "menopausal" by doctors and treated accordingly, when menopause may not be the cause of their ills at all.

While the changes a woman may undergo during menopause should not be defined as trivial, the climacteric usually occurs without difficulty (Troll and Turner, 1978). Where negative psychological symptoms do occur, they are generally related to marital stress, low self-esteem, or other similar factors that happen to coincide with, but are not caused by, the menopause.

The myths and stereotypes surrounding this phase of adulthood will not be rejected until women begin to understand the physical and emotional changes that accompany this normal process called menopause.

What Is Menopause?

Menopause means *cessation of menses* and is one component in the *climacteric*, the entire process of gradual transition from reproduction to nonreproduction. ("Climacteric" is Greek and means, literally, "rung of the ladder.") The climacteric involves three phases, which are characterized by physicians as premenopausal, menopausal, and postmenopausal. The climacteric usually lasts 10 years, from ages 45 to 55, and results from changes in the body's regulatory processes.

The more important regulatory influences emanate from the higher levels of the brain, especially the hypothalamus and the cerebral cortex. A nerve tract passes from the hypothalamus through the pituitary stalk to the cells of the posterior lobe. The hypothalamus secretes hormones that travel to the pituitary gland and are stored there until needed. Among these are the gonadotropic hormones, which are directly involved in the processes of menstruation and menopause. Gonadotropic hormones have two roles. They maintain the production of gametes (sperm and ova) and they stimulate the secretion of sex hormones.

In females, the activities of the ovary are controlled by these gonadotropic hormones. One of them, called the follicle stimulating hormone (FSH), stimulates the maturation process in the follicles. However, FSH by itself does not induce ovulation. A second hormone, luteinising hormone (LH), is required. This hormone, in combination with FSH, stimulates secretion of estrogens by the follicle and brings the follicle to the state at which ovulation occurs. In addition, LH is required for the development of the corpus luteum and the secretion of progesterone.

In the normal menstrual cycle, FSH is released by the pituitary gland, causing the maturity and release of eggs (ova). The ova, in turn, cause the release of progesterone, which causes estrogen levels to rise. The estrogen causes menstruation (endometrial bleeding). During the premenopausal state, the ovaries are increasingly less responsive to FSH. This lessened responsiveness to FSH leads to a reduction in the number of ova released. The reduction of progesterone levels are not sufficient to increase estrogen to a level where bleeding will occur, resulting in a "skipped" menstrual period. The hypothalamus may then overreact, producing excessive FSH in order to stimulate the ovaries and reestablish the usual cyclic feedback of estrogen and progesterone.

The outward signs of these hormone changes are irregular menstrual periods. The most usual pattern involves a lighter and lighter flow each period with a longer and longer interval between periods, although some women will experience shorter intervals and heavier flow.

Symptoms of Menopause

The *average* age of menopause in the United States is 50. Menopause is considered to have occurred when 12 consecutive months have passed without a period.

A number of symptoms accompany the menopause, although only two, hot flashes and vaginal atrophy, are thought to be directly related to decreased estrogen levels. All women do not necessarily experience menopausal symptoms. The Women's Medical Center (1977) estimates that 20 percent of women have no symptoms at all, and 15 percent experience symptoms of a severe nature, warranting treatment. The majority of women (65 percent) have mild symptoms and are able to cope with them without medical intervention.

The *hot flash* is the most commonly reported symptom associated with menopause, and is an unexpected, uncontrollable, but brief, wave of heat that sweeps over the woman's body. Especially severe cases leave the woman soaked with perspiration. Hot flashes can be explained by understanding the mechanism by which body temperature is regulated.

Control of body temperature depends on the hypothalamus. The hypothalamus responds to heat and acts to increase heat loss in two ways. One of these involves sweat secretion, which increases heat loss by evaporation. The second involves dilation of blood vessels in the skin, which causes the surface temperature of the body to approximate the core temperature, with the result that more heat is lost by conduction and evaporation. The hypothalamus also responds to cold by increasing heat production. Blood vessels in the skin constrict, minimizing heat exchange between the core and the cool surfaces of the body. Chilling causes shivering and a hormonal discharge that increases body metabolism, and consequently, heat production.

During a hot flash, inaccurate signals are sent to the hypothalamus. The hormone to increase body metabolism is activated, and the resultant heat production causes the hot flash, which can last from several seconds to several minutes. The woman rarely flushes or shows any outward sign of the flash of internal heat.

Vaginal atrophy seems to be directly related to lower estrogen levels. The inner lining of the vagina becomes drier, thinner, and less elastic. This can lead to painful intercourse for some women. A pattern of regular sexual activity reduces the incidence of painful intercourse. Estrogen deficiency also affects the secondary sex characteristics of postmenopausal women. Skin tone and elasticity are lost, resulting in facial wrinkles and sagging breasts.

Other symptoms, such as thinning hair, weight gain, headaches, insomnia, dizziness, nausea, osteoporosis, and atherosclerosis, have not been directly linked to menopause. Rather, these symptoms are related to other aging processes or physiological problems. Symptoms of depression, nervousness, irritability, and anxiety are believed to result from a woman's psychological problems with aging, rather than from a physiological base. Labeling requirements for estrogen, established by the Food and Drug Administration, state that ". . . there is no evidence that estrogen is effective for nervous symptoms or depression . . . and it should not be used to treat these symptoms."

Estrogen Replacement Therapy

One of the most controversial aspects of menopause involves the decrease in natural estrogen levels and estrogen replacement therapy (ERT). ERT involves replacing the estrogen that a woman's body no longer produces, and is usually prescribed for severe cases. Estrogen has been proven highly successful in relieving hot flashes and vaginal atrophy; as a result, ERT has been welcomed by women.

Estrogen is usually taken in the form of a pill. The most common form of estrogen used in ERT is "conjugated estrogen equine," a mixture of natural estrogens obtained from the urine of pregnant mares. It differs from birth control pills, which contain synthetic estrogens. Estrogen is an extremely powerful substance. A complete physical examination and checkups at six-month intervals, including a pelvic and breast examination, are usually required by physicians prescribing estrogen. Estrogen is usually not prescribed for women with a history of blood-clotting, abnormal genital bleeding, hypertension, heart condition, fibroid tumors, stroke, sickle cell anemia, or with suspected breast or uterine cancer. When estrogen is prescribed, the pills are generally taken for three weeks, followed by a one-week rest. The pills are available in four strengths, and only the lowest dosage necessary to relieve symptoms should be prescribed.

The use of ERT is highly controversial since the true relationship between estrogen and cancer has not been satisfactorily determined. It has been known for 30 years that estrogens, at both high and low doses, cause cancer in test animals. It is also known that, in humans, estrogens can stimulate existing cancer of the breast, uterus, cervix, and vagina.

Despite reports that contend that ERT, when properly administered, does not cause uterine or breast cancer, and may even offer protection against them, the FDA warns on labels of conjugated estrogen medication that the chances for uterine cancer increase five to seven times with ERT. A recent Johns Hopkins study (Antunes et al., 1979) estimates the risk of uterine malignancy to be six times higher among users of estrogen, and 15 times higher if estrogen has been used for more than five years.

For women on ERT, then, the danger of cancer is real. The words of Dr. Roy Hertz, former Chief of Endocrinology of the National Cancer Institute, should give us pause: "Our inadequate knowledge concerning the relationship of estrogen to cancer in women is comparable with what was known about the association between lunger cancer and cigarette smoking before extensive study delineated this overwhelmingly significant relationship" (Corea, 1978).

The FDA does classify estrogen as effective in the treatment of hot flashes and recommends short-term treatment when estrogen is prescribed for that purpose. Despite this recommendation, the average amount of time spent on ERT by most women is ten years (Corea, 1978). Even though ERT is effective in ameliorating hot flashes, women so affected must determine for themselves whether the condition is serious enough to warrant the use of a drug that causes cancer in animals and is associated with increased risk of cancer in women.

Menopause and Depression

While menopause does not *cause* depression, it can have a strong impact at a time when other factors are at work. Because menopause occurs at the time when some women are losing their full-time jobs as mothers and also as wives, because many middle-aged career husbands are experiencing pressures to excel at the office and so have little time to offer emotional support at home, and because the middle-aged woman is told in not-so-subtle ways that she is no longer appealing in a culture that values youth and beauty, it is not uncommon for these women to feel depressed. It is very easy to blame menopause rather than the negative cultural biases related to these life changes for this depression, because the menopause is such an obvious physical manifestation of a change and occurs at the same time. There is little doubt that depression is a major problem for women of middle age; suicide rates for women peak between the ages of 45 and 55 (Kimmel, 1974). Men do not exhibit a sharp increase in suicide rates until age 65 and older.

Despite social stereotyping and medical bias regarding the climacteric, many older women approach menopause with a positive outlook. Few middle-aged women, as compared with young women, view the menopause as a significant event (Neugarten et al., 1968). Many menopausal and postmenopausal women believe that going through the menopause does not change a woman in any important way and that women who have trouble during menopause are those who are expecting it.

Although not empirically tested, there appears to be a relationship between activity level and psychological symptoms. Women who are involved in careers or leisure pursuits and who derive intrinsic satisfaction from those activities do not seem to experience the severe psychological symptoms of menopause. It is as if they have neither the time nor the inclination to be bothered. Or, the very fact that they are so active means that they are already in good shape, physiologically and psychologically.

Hysterectomy: Artificial Menopause

A simple hysterectomy is an operation to remove the uterus and cervix; a total hysterectomy also involves removal of the ovaries and the fallopian tubes. Removal of the ovaries causes surgical or artificial menopause, since estrogen levels are curtailed. Symptoms related to surgical menopause are the same as those caused by a normal menopause.

Removal of ovaries (oophorectomy) is often recommended in women past 40 who are undergoing hysterectomy. This recommendation results from American Cancer Society estimates that 1 percent of women over 40 will develop ovarian cancer. The cure rate for women who do get ovarian cancer is low—only 10 to 20 percent. According to Paulshock (1976), "ovarian carcinoma is particularly deadly because it is extremely difficult to diagnose before it metastasizes or spreads beyond the ovary" (p. 26). Because more than 80 percent of women with ovarian cancer have already had a hysterectomy, doctors increasingly are encouraging oophorectomy at the time of hysterectomy.

Hysterectomy is the most commonly performed operation in the United States (Morgan, 1978; Paulshock, 1976). In 1968 more than half a million (545,000) operations were performed. By 1977 the number rose to 800,000, a 47 percent increase. The rate is steadily climbing; if increases persist, 40 percent of American women will have a hysterectomy by age 40, and 50 percent by age 65.

Reasons for Hysterectomy Although many women assume that hysterectomy is performed only in cases of cancer, there are a number of reasons doctors recommend this surgical procedure. The greatest number of hysterectomies are performed to correct pelvic relaxation or *uterine prolapse*. Problems arise when the uterus loosens from its proper position within the body and slips in the vaginal tract. This condition is common to women who have had several children, since pregnancy stretches the ligaments that hold the uterus in place.

The next most common reason for hysterectomy is elimination of *fibroid tumors*. These tumors are fairly common; one out of four women get them (Morgan, 1978). They are not cancerous and do not necessarily create problems. Hysterectomy is recommended when fibroid tumors cause abnormal bleeding, "bleeding that occurs at times other than when it is expected during the menstrual cycle" (Paulshock, 1976, p. 25), or when they grow large enough to cause abdominal pain or pressure.

The third most common reason for hysterectomy is *cancer*. As with fibroid tumors, abnormal bleeding is symptomatic of a problem. Because the Pap test can detect cancer at a very early stage, uterine cancer is not necessarily life threatening.

Other reasons for hysterectomy are *endometriosis* (growth of uterine tissue where it does not belong, such as on the ovaries or tubes or on the ligaments holding the uterus); *pelvic inflammatory disease* (a bacterial infection that attacks the tubes and ovaries); and *sterilization* (usually performed on poor or retarded women, and very seldom medically necessary).

Surgery and the Older Woman   In terms of risk, hysterectomy is a fairly safe operation. The mortality rate for this procedure is less than 2 deaths per 1,000 women (Paulshock, 1976). Because *any* surgery entails some degree of danger, there are few gynecologic operations performed on patients 75 to 80 years old. Many surgeons are hesitant to operate on a patient after age 80 for anything less than a lifesaving procedure (Ballard, 1969).

Following a study of 195 cases of major gynecologic surgery performed on women 65 years of age and older, McKeithen (1975) concluded that the elderly female patient can tolerate such surgery very well in a modern-day hospital setting. "The patient who is senile, semi-invalid, and hesitant about surgery is the one to think twice about before operating" (McKeithen, 1975, p. 63).

Osteoporosis

Osteoporosis affects millions of women; postmenopausal osteoporosis alone affects more than 6 million women (Alvarez, 1970). The condition is characterized by increased porousness of the bone, resulting in extreme fragility. The high incidence of bone fractures in the aged population can be explained by this condition.

"The literature of the last three decades is full of contradictory theories as to the cause and treatment of osteoporosis" (Tonna, 1977, p. 477). Because osteoporosis occurs primarily in postmenopausal women, it has been thought to be related to decreasing estrogen levels characteristic of such women. While such a relationship is postulated, the mechanism responsible for changes in bone density remains unclear to medical researchers. Without knowledge of the cause, successful treatment is unknown, although estrogen replacement therapy is a commonly employed routine.

The effect of ERT on osteoporosis is controversial. While ERT has arrested osteoporosis, the period of remission is fairly short, usually three to nine months, after which time the condition resumes (Boston Women's Health Book Collective, 1976). Others, who feel that osteoporosis is not the result of reduced estrogen, but rather the consequence of poor calcium and protein intake and insufficient exercise, advocate a high calcium and high protein diet as treatment.

SEXUALITY AFTER 40

In terms of appearance and sexuality, there exists what Sontag (1972) has termed a "double standard of aging." Despite the physiological truth that women are capable of engaging in sexual activity well into old age, both males and females accept the social belief that after the early or mid-40s, women are no longer sexually attractive and therefore no longer interested in sex. Traditionally, a woman's status has been based on her physical appearance and sexuality. As she aged, her worth declined.

This contrasts sharply with the cultural notion that males in their 40s are still sexually desirable. Since a man's status has long been defined in terms of personality, intelligence, career achievement, and earning power, his worth and thus his sexuality do not diminish until his mid-60s when he retires. At that point, the image of the asexual, undesirable older woman is balanced by the image of the sexually alive but equally undesirable "dirty old man."

In our culture, women are defined as "undesirable" some 20 years earlier, chronologically, than are men. Men can marry women 15 to 20 years younger but not 5 or more years older.

Female sexuality after middle age has been long ignored as a research topic because most investigators already "knew" there was nothing to research. This cultural bias is exemplified by responses to sentence-completion questionnaires administered to students at a northeastern university. The stem "Sex for most older people is . . ." elicited "negligible," "unimportant," and "past" as responses from most of the students.

There are a number of reasons for the strong disapproval of sexual activity in older men and women. Americans share the attitude that aging is a disease rather than a normal process. "Sick" people are not supposed to exhibit any desire for sex, nor do we think of sick people as sexually attractive. This social attitude is further exacerbated by an emphasis in both research literature and popular articles on the small percentage of older adults who are sick and inactive, instead of on the majority who are healthy and involved. Despite the fact that only 5 percent of individuals over the age of 65 live in nursing homes or other similar institutions, the stereotype of the senile old person in a nursing home persists. Since menopause is viewed as the onset of aging in women, and since psychological evidence of aging is viewed as a pathological condition, it follows that women are expected to conform to the asexual role that is socially prescribed. Further, many of today's older women grew up in a time when "nice" girls or women didn't think about, talk about, or desire sex.

A second reason for the disapproval of sexual activity in older people lies in the American tradition of equating sex and love with youth. As women approach middle-age and menopause, biological changes equated with aging become evident. These include graying hair, wrinkling skin, and a "settling" of body weight. Because women begin to look "old," they are treated as such by both younger individuals and by men of like or greater age.

A third reason is fed by the notion that sex is procreative rather than recreative. Since women are no longer capable of bearing children much beyond their early 50s, there is no "need" for sex, hence there must be no desire. In fact, there can be a dramatic shift in orientation toward, and quality of, sexual activity for women in their mid-years and beyond. The elimination after menopause of fear of pregnancy can be liberating to a large number of women. Many women indicate an improvement in sexual activity because they no longer have concerns about unwanted pregnancies.

Studies of female sexuality negate the image of the asexual older woman. In his study of sexual behavior in the female, Kinsey (1953) noted a gradual decline in the frequency of sexual intercourse between ages of 20 and 60, but felt that it resulted from aging in the male. There was little evidence of any aging in the sexual capacities of the female until late in her life. Similarly, Masters and Johnson (1966) discovered that for women over 60 capacity to reach orgasm was not diminished.

In fact, sexual *activity* declines with age for women because available partners become scarce. Sexual *interest* does not reflect any decline. Those women who enjoyed sex as young adults continue to enjoy it as middle-aged and aged adults. A regular pattern of sexual activity has been described by some researchers as a correlate to continued vitality.

A longitudinal study, conducted at Duke University, compared male and female sexual activity. Of the males who indicated an *interest* in sex, 87 percent were sexually active. Only 60 percent of the women who expressed an interest in sex were sexually active. Ten years later, however, only 31 percent of these same men were still sexually active, while no change was recorded for the women. Even after a decade, 60 percent were sexually active. Seventy-five percent of the couples involved in this study, both males and females, tended to agree that the husbands were responsible for the cessation of intercourse. It would appear, then, that as long as an interested, capable partner is available, women are interested and engage in sexual activity with little or no decline.

Breast Cancer

Breast cancer is an issue of increasing concern to women as they age because greater numbers of older women encounter this health problem with each succeeding generation. Since 1965 the number of reported cases has increased by 50 percent. Despite dramatic improvements in medicine and health education over the last 50 years, the death rate for breast cancer is virtually the same as it was in 1930.

One out of every fifteen women in the United States between the ages of 35 and 55 develops breast cancer. The disease rarely develops in girls under 20, and until recently it was seldom found before 30. For unknown reasons, when it occurs before age 30 it is more virulent than in the case with older women. The incidence peaks between the ages of 42 and 47; then an eight-year plateau is evident. Starting in the early 50s the rate again climbs, though not as steeply, until very old age.

Many experts interpret this as statistical support for the belief that many breast cancers in young women are different diseases than those found in older women. This theory received support from American investigators in a study published in 1974 by three Johns Hopkins researchers (Craig, Comstock, and Geiser, 1974). The study reported a distinct difference in the histories and risk factors of women who developed breast cancer before age 45 and women who developed it later in life. According to their findings, a family history of breast cancer and later age of the birth of the first child were more often associated with the disease in younger women, while breast feeding was thought to be a factor with the older women.

Many women think that the risk of getting breast cancer disappears after age 70. This is not true. The total number of new cases does drop with age, because fewer women are still alive, but the incidence rate among women over 70 actually increases.

It is thought that breast cancer may begin to develop as many as 20 years before a tumor becomes detectable. Most breast cancer cases are diagnosed after discovery of a lump. By the time a tumor is detected this way, the patient may have had the disease for a decade.

Studies of female hormones have suggested that changing hormonal balance may also play a part in determining cancer risk. Women produce at least three forms of estrogen, the major hormone secreted during the reproductive years. One form is predominant in populations with a low risk of breast cancer, while another is more common in populations with a high risk. Thus, Asian women, with a high estrogen balance, have a low risk of breast cancer, while American women, with a low estrogen balance, have a high risk of breast cancer. Interestingly, Asian women living in Hawaii have a moderate estrogen balance and a moderate chance of getting the disease. This suggests that environment, and particularly diet, may play as crucial a role as heredity in determining potential risk, since the Asian women in Hawaii were "Americanized."

Only within the past few years has much attention been paid to the possible role of the environment in breast cancer. Environmental factors appear to have the greatest impact during two periods in a woman's life: adolescence (menarche) and middle-age (menopause). During the critical years at both ends of a woman's reproductive life, environmental factors may interact with the genes to produce disease.

Diet has been a proven factor in cancer in animal studies, where high-fat diets hasten tumor development. There is also a direct correlation between the breast cancer rate in a country and the amount of fat in the local diet.

The several identified patterns of breast tissue, ranging from fine, threadlike, uniform milk ducts to thick, beaded, irregular ducts and modular glands, also seem to bear a relationship to breast cancer risk. The fine pattern offers the least risk to the disease, while the thick pattern offers the highest risk. Adolescents tend to have the thicker, high-risk pattern of breast tissue, but adulthood is usually accompanied by a change to one of the finer, lower-risk patterns.

Women More Likely to Develop Breast Cancer   Who are the women most likely to develop breast cancer? The highest risk category of all is made up of the women who have already had one cancerous breast removed. They are the most likely to develop a malignancy in the other breast. Overall, in the United States, white women have a higher incidence than women of other races. Surveys indicate that being black appears to be a protection.

But as blacks climb in socioeconomic status, the incidence increases as their life style changes.

Being overweight is another factor that increases the risk of developing a malignant tumor. Also, excess fatty tissue can make it more difficult to find one that is already there. It is possible that a history of benign disease, such as cystic mastitis or multiple benign tumors of the ducts, increases the chances of getting breast cancer.

Cancer frequently runs in families. This issue is debated by scientists who argue about genetics and heredity. But the risk is higher if a mother, sister, or maternal grandmother has had breast cancer. One specialist feels that the important factor is the age of a woman's mother or sister at the time either developed her disease.

Women who begin menstruating at an early age are more likely to develop breast cancer. Early menarche presupposes a long reproductive life. On the other hand, if a woman has her ovaries removed before she is 35, or has a natural menopause at an early age, her chances of developing breast cancer drop. A woman whose first full-term child was born before she was 20 (age applies only in the United States) has substantially reduced her risk of developing breast cancer. At the other end of the age line, a woman who has her first child after 35 has elevated her risk. There seems to be little question that women who have no children are in the high-risk category. There is controversy about whether breast-feeding protects against breast cancer. Some data refute the relationship, while other data support it.

There is one factor that appears to prevent cancer of the breast; removal of the ovaries before the age of 40. If the uterus was removed along with the ovaries, and small doses of estrogen were given continuously, there would be no cyclic stimulation of the breast by hormones. Without stimulation, there would be reduced reproduction of breast cells and perhaps a reduced incidence of cancer, for a cell that does not divide cannot give rise to a cancer cell.

Adjustment to Breast Cancer   Despite the fact that greater proportions of older women encounter breast cancer with each succeeding generation, little has been written outside of medical textbooks. A woman's breasts have long been considered a symbol of her sexuality. Because breast cancer is usually treated by surgery, mastectomy (the removal of a portion or all of the breast) can have a strong psychological impact, in addition to causing physical trauma.

A survey done by Kushner (1975) found that young married women were not as horrified by the loss of a breast as *postmenopausal married women,* whose youth and sexual attractiveness have begun to fade (or so they think). These women are far more vulnerable to psychological problems because they tend to have emotional troubles at this time of life even without the loss of a breast. Their children may no longer be living at home; their husbands may show little concern for them. Women feel that they have lost their jobs and that they are losing their womanliness. Then, on top of this, the pain and strain of breast cancer and mastectomy are added.

The emotional condition of older married women seems to depend on the status of their marriages. Losing a breast causes a more severe psychological jolt for women with bad marriages than for women with good marriages. Where divorce occurs directly following surgery, the marriage was generally already finished, and the mastectomy is only an excuse to get out of a situation that was already bad.

Older women who have never married seem to make the best adjustment of all to breast removal. Most of them long ago gave up any concern about "catching" a man, and their self-image is not as tightly connected to their bodies. Moreover, unmarried older women tend to continue close relationships with family and old friends. Among these women, however, the fear of dying is a very close and real dread. By the time a woman reaches 65 or 70, she has probably witnessed the painful deaths of many friends and relations. It does little good to tell her that doctors now have ways to alleviate the pain she considers to be part of dying from breast cancer. Her anxieties are mainly concerned with the pain associated with the disease.

In terms of marital status and age, the women who respond to mastectomy with the greatest stress are in their 50s or older and are either widowed or divorced. Their desire to ignore the tumor completely, to have a lumpectomy or partial mastectomy, or to investigate plastic surgery is greater than in other groups.

In the 1974 Gallup Poll it was reported that breast loss can affect both a woman's self-image and her relations with men. This attitude is most common among single women and those between 18 and 34 years of age. It has also been found, to no one's surprise, that although women worry about the loss of their femininity, their main concern is that all the cancer has been removed and that they will not die.

In general, the psychological status of the woman has a lot to do with her physical recovery, assuming she does not develop metastic disease. Women who know in advance that they are to have mastectomies, who have some input into the decision making, and who do not feel duped by the doctor tend to recover more quickly and easily in every respect. Those women for whom the mastectomy comes as a surprise take longer to heal physically and emotionally. Overall there is no set pattern for either mental or physical recovery. Each woman seems to proceed at her own pace.

Our culture has made a woman's breast a significant status symbol. Dr. Philip Strax (1974) writes:

> We live in a breast-oriented society. To the average woman, her breast is the badge of femininity, an important part of her allurement to charm her male. To the man, the breast is a source of excitement, an erotic stimulation. It has become a bridge between male and female and is used as a reward to be flaunted before the eyes of the male in the female's attempt to attract him. This emphasis on the breast as a sex symbol begins in adolescence and apparently persists throughout life.

Much of this is caused by the influence of the media, magazines, book jackets, and billboards. To be sexy a woman must have voluptuous breasts. The media, largely made up of men, has made the breast into the ultimate erotic symbol. Thus, it is not surprising to discover that loss of a breast is equated by many men and women with loss of sexuality.

SUMMARY

The related topics of menopause and sexuality continue to be poorly understood by women experiencing physiological change and by the practitioners to whom women turn for professional advice. Menopause is the result of hormonal change, the external sign of which is a change in menstrual flow until 12 months have passed without a menstrual period. At that point menopause has occurred.

Contrary to myths and stereotypes about the consequences of menopause, hot flashes and vaginal atrophy are the only two symptoms directly linked to the menopause. While these can be controlled with estrogen replacement therapy, ERT is a highly controversial matter since its relationship to cancer has not been determined beyond a reasonable doubt.

Hysterectomy, the most commonly performed operation in the United States, can be thought of as an artificial menopause. Symptoms related to hysterectomy are the same as those caused by menopause.

Osteoporosis, a bone condition affecting millions of older women, is thought to be strongly related to the decrease in estrogen that occurs after natural or artificial menopause. Thus, ERT has been used in an attempt to reverse this condition.

Sexuality does not decline as a result of the menopause. In fact, many women indicate an improvement in the quality of their sexual lives because they no longer are faced with the fear of unwanted pregnancies.

Breast cancer is a medical issue with strong psychological overtones because American culture has made a woman's breast the ultimate symbol of sexuality. Many older women mistakenly believe that the loss of a breast is equated with loss of sexuality, and so have also subscribed to the myth of the asexual older woman so prevalent among younger individuals.

The physiological changes wrought by the aging process in women and the psychological adjustments required by menopause and a changing view of sexuality are areas that are little understood, and will require close scrutiny in the years ahead.

■4
Mental Health
and Related Issues

The mental health needs of older women are different from those of older people in general. Too often, generalizations have been offered to account for the psychological ills of the elderly population as a whole, without concern for the differences attributable to sex. Just as it would be inadvisable to assume that the only thing older men and older women have in common is age, so, too, is it inappropriate to assume that the mental health problems of older men and older women can be dealt with in the same manner. In this chapter, we will examine age-related correlates of stress and depression. Both adequate and inadequate coping mechanisms are also presented.

Recent investigations are evidence of the increasing recognition of, and interest in, older women and their uniqueness, even in terms of mental health. Depression, stress, suicide, drug abuse, and alcoholism can be found in both older men and women, but significant differences have been reported on the basis of sex. Older women have their own mechanisms for coping with psychological woes. They undergo changes that are unique to their sex, changes that in many cases will greatly affect their existence, and they must prevail in their attempts to be recognized by the psychological community as having special needs.

CHANGES IN OLDER WOMEN

Older women today are apt to be confronted with changes that, at times, appear to be insurmountable. With all of the required emotional adjustments women must make, their longer life spans appear all the more surprising. One explanation for their longevity is that women become so accustomed to adapting to new events in their lives, they can accept change in their later years with little difficulty (Saul, 1974).

One such change involves the role of motherhood. As children grow up and move out of their parents' house to be on their own, the mother, anywhere in age from her late 30s on up, finds herself facing the loss of a valued role. This major change, leaving many women with a great deal of empty time on their hands, may lead to serious and unsettling emotional responses.

Another adjustment that women face is the changing perception, theirs and society's, of the role of housewife. When nonemployed women refer to themselves as *"just* a housewife," it is clear their self-evaluation is low. Older women who have spent the greater portion of their lives in this occupation, without pay, and now without prestige, must find some way of dealing with this attack on their self-esteem for which nothing in their experience has prepared them.

Many older women must also learn to cope with the loss of a spouse, either through divorce or death. Divorce, after 15 to 25 years of marriage, drastically alters a woman's life. Despite research that suggests that older men may suffer more on the loss of a spouse (Lowenthal and Haven, 1968), widowhood also brings severe upheaval into a woman's life. In contrast to older men, older women turn to relatives and organizations in which they are members in times of such need. Older men have a greater opportunity for remarriage, as pointed out earlier, so their sufferings might be greater but of a shorter duration than those of women, who face a future with no hope for the renewal and support of marital intimacy.

Older women who are alone face the very real possibility of being social isolates. The physical and biological changes in aging women make them less valued and therefore less acceptable socially, and subsequently less acceptable to themselves. Avoiding the loss of social esteem drives some older women to excessive, and inevitably unsuccessful, use of devices to produce a youthful appearance. All of these processes have implications for the mental health of older women.

While many women may try to mask the outward physical effects of aging, there is little they can do about the physiological changes that are taking place inside their bodies. Every woman who has reached old age has had to go through menopause or, as it is significantly, if inappropriately, labeled, the "change of life." The stigma associated with this "change has brought despair to many women" (Women's Medical Center, 1977).

Changes in physical health can also affect mental health in older women. Older women with physical ailments that limit their activities and older women anticipating such problems certainly have a greater chance of developing some type of psychological difficulty. Older women facing loss of hearing, diminished sight, or diminished mobility may find it difficult to cope without the benefit of external intervention.

Older women have another burden to deal with: trying to survive on a meager or less-than-adequate income. Most older women do manage to endure the change in economic status. Some older women try to improve their financial status by looking for employment. In so doing they are further reminded of the restrictions imposed on them by society, for they find employment opportunities extremely limited, in large part because of their age.

One impending change that strongly influences the mental state of the older woman is death. Most older women either reach some sort of acceptance of its imminence or avoid the subject entirely and go on with the task of living. There are other older women for whom the thought of death is so trying that they have difficulty leading a normal life.

Most older women will encounter variations of these changes as they age. Some women may endure all of these changes with grace, equanimity, and serenity. For other women, only one of these events might trigger emotional dysfunction. There is little doubt that most older women have suffered some degree of stress as a result of these changes, which in total are "changes in life."

Overall satisfaction with life is generally recognized to be an important component in determining mental health. "Poor health, low income, and lack of social interaction, among other things, are clearly related to lower expressed satisfaction with life, lower morale, and lower contentment" (Larson, 1978, p. 109). In surveying 30 years of research on well-being as judged by the older persons themselves, Larson (1978) found no consistent evidence of sex differences in well-being for older people. Studies that differentiated various marital statuses suggested that single and married persons were roughly equivalent in their level of reported well-being, while the level of widowed, separated, and divorced persons tended to be lower.

Because widowhood is likely to be a part of many women's lives, well-being in relation to widowhood is important to consider. Arens (1979) found that low economic resources create the main adverse effect on the well-being of widows, as compared with lower social participation as the main adverse effect on the well-being of widowers.

STRESS

Stress is not simply the result of factors that create worry, anxiety, or strain. Stress reactions within the body can be created when a person has to make a change or adaptation in his or her life, whether positive or negative. A pleasant event such as a vacation still requires a person to make adjustments that may induce stress. When too many adjustments are required over a short period of time, stress and tension result.

"Basically, when human beings are subjected to major stress, they are roused to a fight-or-flight reaction in the same way that animals are" (Pelletier, 1977, p. 69). However, in our society fighting or running away is not considered an appropriate reaction to stress. Instead, a person learns to internalize such reactions and to respond in a calm, dignified manner. The body is in a state of stress reactivity, while outwardly the person strives to appear calm. Because no action is taken, the stress response continues. Prolonged, unabated stress is the primary contributing factor for the development of cardiovascular disorders, cancer, arthritis, and respiratory diseases. These diseases affect mainly older people, and older women in particular because of their greater life expectancy.

The stress-reaction system within the body is needed to cope effectively with life situations. With an opportunity to define and react to a particular source of stress, the body can recover and return to normal functioning. Frequently, however, sources of stress in our daily lives are ambiguous or prolonged, so there is little opportunity for the person to identify and recover from the stress-alarm reaction that various stresses induce.

Excessive levels of stress within the lives of older women can occur for many different reasons. As discussed in the previous section, older women today are faced with adjustment to changing values concerning women's roles, as well as changing circumstances created by factors such as retirement, widowhood, or divorce.

Middle age can be a period in a woman's life that may threaten her very existence. The changing status of the older woman's social roles, as well as the outer and inner physical manifestations of the aging process, all work to affect her outlook on life. Anxieties and tension develop from conflicts over identity and purpose and the physical reminders of age and approaching death.

If the older woman's self-evaluation reveals an unsatisfying past and present life, she will find it difficult to summon the emotional strength to deal with daily routines. If the older woman successfully survives these stressful situations, she will be better able to cope with future stressful situations. The older woman who cannot cope will develop serious psychological symptoms. Who are the women overcome by stress, and what makes them different from the women who cope with stress?

Studies have been conducted to determine the characteristics of women who undergo age-related periods of stress. In a review of the literature on sex differences in mental health, it has been pointed out that as women get older they report distress in all areas of behavior. It has also been documented that older women are inclined to admit having problems and to talk about their concerns. Although older women may be subject to stress because they feel inadequate or because of role loss, they appear on the whole able to adapt to stress. Society's expectation and acceptance of a woman's display of emotion may contribute to the ability of women to cope with emotional stress.

In an effort to assess the factors related to stress, one study questioned teachers and nonteachers in a school system. Responses from subjects between the ages of 20 and 65 indicated that while female married teachers experienced an increase in stress in their early 40s, female married nonteachers found the early 50s to be quite stressful. Women of higher socioeconomic status reported feeling less stress than women of lower socioeconomic levels (Horrocks and Mussman, 1970).

The work environment can be another source of stress. A majority of employed women over age 45 are in jobs of a service or clerical nature. Time pressure, conflicts with supervisors and coworkers, and responsibility overload are some factors that can induce stress in the work environment. A study by Levi (1967) demonstrated how time and production pressures created a high level of stress in women in the invoicing department of a large office. The method of pay had been changed from a fixed monthly salary to a piecework rate. Under the piecework rate, production rose substantially, with the incidence of mistakes no greater than usual. However, the women reported many more signs of discomfort, such as pains in various parts of their bodies and almost twice the amount of fatigue. The excretion of stress hormones into the urine was also higher. Excessive strain on the job, along with concentrated periods of life change, are perhaps the most common sources of the type of stress that may eventually induce illness (Pelletier, 1977).

The greater stress imposed on men in our society is thought to be one possible cause of their higher level of cardiovascular disease. Sex hormones have been considered a protective factor for premenopausal women. However, a 1974 study by Friedman and Rosenman found that women in other countries had as high an incidence of heart disease as men and that black women in the United States had a slightly higher susceptibility than black men. These researchers predict that as more and more women enter the work force, their susceptibility to cardiovascular diseases will increase.

Emphasis upon technological innovations in American society encourages people to try to find faster and better ways to carry out their daily tasks. Older women may have multiple responsibilities that they feel the need to handle faster: household routines, job tasks, care of aging parents, and demands of husband and children. They may feel that they should always be engaged in some constructive activity, even during their leisure time. These factors can create a preoccupation with time: a person will think about activities she is going to do or has to do while engaged in another activity (Pelletier, 1977). Such behavior is unnatural and stress-inducing.

Unexpressed anger can be another source of stress. Women now aged 45 and over often have acquired attitudes that encourage them to suppress hostile feelings and blame themselves if situations are resolved in a less-than-satisfying manner. There is considerable evidence that internalized anger induces a prolonged stress reaction, which is more damaging to the body than the short-term strain involved in immediately expressing anger (Pelletier, 1977).

Older women react to stress in a variety of ways. In some cases it has been reported that older women who have been hospitalized for various reasons, and who are under a great amount of stress, exhibit a pattern of gross self-neglect. They may be filthy in appearance, live in squalor, and place themselves in situations where they are more likely to have accidents

(Clark, Manikar, and Gray, 1975). Stress can also lead to other signs of mental problems such as depression, suicide, drug abuse, and alcoholism.

The most common response to stress is to seek relief through the use of alcohol, tranquilizers, and other socially acceptable drugs. This behavior treats the symptoms but ignores the long-term effects of stress on the mind and body. Older women will have to make an effort to gain information about the effect of high stress levels on their physical and mental health. To become more aware of specific sources of stress in their daily lives, they can begin by noting attitudes, actions, and types of situations that create symptoms of discomfort and tension. Learning and practicing meditation and relaxation techniques, such as biofeedback and yoga, can reduce stress and promote a sense of control and effectiveness in handling one's life. Reducing stress to a level that promotes and maintains a state of health often means reevaluating one's attitudes and habits (Pelletier, 1977).

DEPRESSION

Recent research investigations have shown that depression strikes women of all ages, races, and ethnic groups. Depression is no longer the symptom of a middle-age crisis among menopausal women of higher socioeconomic status (Weissman, 1972). It is prevalent in older women, and is one of the leading symptoms in women of all ages who seek professional help for psychological troubles.

There is no way to tell in exact numbers how many or how often older women experience acute depression. Housewives in their 40s and 50s may be overwhelmed by depression, particularly as their children no longer need their help. Depression sets in when these women experience a diminishing responsibility in their roles. Depression occurs more often in middle-aged women than in men; men do not appear to go through the same physiological and social role changes as women as they age (Hargreaves, 1975). Loneliness, despair, and a sense of bereavement on reaching their later years is signified in some women by a loss of appetite, insomnia, loss of interest in people and things, and physical ailments. Other factors can also contribute to depression: genetic predisposition, stressful life events, personality traits, guilt, and frustration (Hargreaves, 1975).

Women may also have a social predisposition for depression. Older women have been socialized to depend on others, and with a decline in female homosociality there is a loss of the vital emotional support once provided by other women.

Marriage, motherhood, work, and socioeconomic status can also be directly tied to depression in women. Marriage may not be a bed of roses; many older women who have been diagnosed as depressed were also married. As the number of elderly women increases, so too will the incidents of depression among them. Few studies deal specifically with depression in elderly women. In 1973 it was reported that 25 percent of the elderly population suffered psychiatric problems (Bennett, 1973). Suggestions were recommended for the treatment of geriatric depression, but age, not sex, was the factor determining the type of care given.

SUICIDE

The suicide rate for elderly women is lower than that for men, which may be one reason why there is little data on the subject. Before age 50, women commit suicide about one-third as often as men, but after that age the rate is only one-tenth that of men (Weiss, 1968).

Between 1953 and 1968 there was a sharp decline in the relationship between age and suicide among women (Atchley, 1974). A similar reduction seems to have occurred in the early 1970s. The suicide rate for women peaks between the ages of 45 and 54, after which there is a steady decline in reported suicides (Kimmel, 1974; Patterson, Abrahams, and Baker, 1974). The peak age for women coincides with such life changes as menopause, children leaving home, divorce, and widowhood. Suicide in older women does occur, however, when depression becomes overwhelming and no intervention occurs.

Studies have confirmed that women make many more attempts at suicide than men, but men complete their attempts more often (Garai, 1970). Women tend to use this method as a cry for help and attention. The elderly, unlike younger people, are extremely successful in carrying out their plans to self-destruct (Patterson, Abrahams, and Baker, 1974). They use methods that are more likely to be fail proof. The data, unfortunately, do not tell us whether or not elderly women are more successful than their younger counterparts in their suicide attempts.

Future research on the elderly must include analyses to identify sex differences, if present. Lacking such analyses, the results can be misleading and confusing. For example, one source (Patterson, Abrahams, and

Baker, 1974) mentions that the suicide rate is lowest for elderly persons who are married. One could conclude, then, that the rates are lowest for elderly men, because most elderly men are married, whereas over half of the elderly women are single. Another study shows that although widowhood *is* directly associated with suicide, widows and wives do not differ significantly in suicide *rate* (Bock and Webber, 1972). Widows with strong attachments to people are less likely to commit suicide than those who have withdrawn from social contact.

In recent years, several authorities (Kastenbaum and Mishara, 1971; Patterson, Abrahams, and Baker, 1974) have asserted that some elderly people are not even aware of their tendency to injure themselves. Older women can do serious harm to themselves (Kastenbaum and Mishara, 1971). Doctors and those close to elderly women and men need to be aware of the following signs of self-destructive tendencies: injuries incurred through accidental falls; unusual weight problems; heavy smoking; failure to plan for and get the proper medical treatment when necessary; delay in getting treatment for cancer; prolonged psychological disturbances; and self-diagnosis and treatment (Patterson, Abrahams, and Baker, 1974). Drug abuse and alcoholism are signals of acute distress in the older woman.

DRUG ABUSE

In the past two decades, there has been a veritable revolution in the development and use of drugs. This has had particular impact on older adults, since approximately 50 percent of the nation's prescription drugs go to that portion of the population over 60 years of age. Although many of the 7,000 drugs prescribed to the middle-aged and elderly are relatively new on the market, most have received little testing on older subjects before marketing. Consequently, little research has been reported on the use of drugs by older adults.

The information that is available does not provide a clear or comprehensive picture of this topic. This situation is worsened by the fact that the interactive effects of the various drugs prescribed to older adults are largely unknown. The use of nonprescription drugs and home remedies further complicates matters. Additionally, the literature on the combined use of prescription drugs with such drugs as nicotine, caffeine, aspirin, and nonprescription analgesics is virtually nonexistent. It is, therefore, understandable that the facts about drug abuse in older women are extremely limited. Despite the limitations in the research, preliminary findings suggest that older women have a problem with drugs.

Use of psychotropic drugs is increasing among the current cohort of older adults and particularly among older women. The increased use is not limited to residents of nursing homes, but is experienced by community-dwelling people as well (Butler, 1975). The elderly are increasing their use of drugs more rapidly than the general population (Wynne and Heller, 1973). Many elderly have problems stemming from social forces, problems leading to loneliness, boredom, rolelessness, lack of mobility, and low incomes (Kimmel, 1974). When these and other problems lead to depression, psychopharmaceuticals, rather than community action or psychotherapy, are often chosen as therapy (Lifshitz and Kline, 1961). Sedatives, tranquilizers, barbiturates, and amphetamines are available either through prescription or over the counter (OTC). Next to cardiovascular drugs, sedatives and tranquilizers are the category of prescription drugs most frequently used by older adults.

Overuse and Misuse of Drugs

One in three suicides in the United States is accomplished by use of prescription drugs; this type of suicide is increasing at a faster rate than is the population (Benson and Brodie, 1975). Twenty-five percent of suicide victims are elderly (Bourne, 1973; Patterson, Abrahams, and Baker, 1974; Resnik and Cantor, 1970). Generally, more females than males are admitted to hospitals for this type of self-poisoning (Bean, 1973), and more unmarried elderly commit suicide (Patterson, Abrahams, and Baker, 1974). Those attempting suicide and admitted to hospitals mostly use sedatives, hypnotics, and other psychotherapeutics in their suicide attempts (Bean, 1973; Bourne, 1973; Burrows and Harari, 1974; Irey and Froede, 1974). Use of a drug for suicide correlates with the current popularity of that drug among prescribing physicians (Bourne, 1973; Burrows and Harari, 1974).

Accidental self-poisoning may be a complication resulting from the taking of drugs in combination. Sedatives, tranquilizers, and antidepressants are frequently used in combination and can inhibit or intensify each other's activity (Learoyd, 1972). Drug effects vary with age; with age, depressants, for example, become more effective and stimulants less so (Bender, 1970; Lenhart, 1976). This varying physiological effect can be harmful and is still being researched.

One recent study (Peterson and Thomas, 1975) examined the records

■5
Life Situations

A great many older American women "are underemployed, underpaid, underfinanced, underhoused, undervalued, and underloved, sometimes even by themselves" (Jacobs, 1976, p. 34). Widowhood, divorce, and abandonment are fairly common experiences that may in the present day befall almost any woman at some point in her life. A woman's fate in our society is no longer so completely tied to that of her husband to the point where the two may be treated as one inseparable entity in terms of economics and status (Amundsen, 1971).

This chapter first examines the transitions encountered by women as they age and the effect that role changes and personality types have in creating a variety of life situations. Then the effects, positive or negative, of social networks, friendship patterns, and living arrangements on women's life situations are described. Lastly, major concerns of older women and societal changes that have the possibility for support and enrichment of women's lives are presented.

The life situations of women over age 40 vary greatly. One situation is that of the married woman who has been a homemaker all her life. As her children grow up and leave home, she will have freedom from child care responsibilities and may have increased financial security. Another example of a life situation is that of the professional woman approaching retirement age who is faced with the adjustment to the loss of a lifetime's pattern of work.

TRANSITIONS

The average life expectancy for a woman at the turn of the century was 47 years. The picture today is dramatically different. "We are the first women to face several decades of living after our traditional roles of wives and mothers have been completed, decades in which we *should* have the opportunity to forge a new and fulfilling life for ourselves" (Collins, 1976, p. 64). The woman who no longer has children at home is forced to redirect her energies. For this woman, replenishment of purpose in the second half of life is gained through "cultivating talents left half finished, permitting ambitions once piggybacked, becoming aggressive in the service of her own convictions rather than a passive-aggressive party to someone else's" (Sheehy, 1976, p. 294).

Older women may restructure their life goals to allow more focus on self and less responsibility for others. A 60-year-old married woman who has been a homemaker and volunteer community worker describes her new focus on self :

> I feel that life under my own steam, in my own control is just beginning. It is exhilarating. I use my energies now for my own self-development and fulfillment. I am becoming a one-person do-it-myself authority on anything that concerns me—health, education, entertainment, adventure, relationships. . . . I feel liberated from a long, sticky period of role playing, stage-managed by everyone but myself, and am now moving into a period of being and becoming myself—which is unfolding and surprising me at every turn: so far, pleasantly, although not without serious confrontations with my husband about my "right" to do so. These confrontations have been to a large degree successful, although involving inevitable compromise on both sides . . . (Collins, 1976, p. 6).

A woman of 64 describes herself and her friends as becoming more and more themselves:

> I have found the greatest joy is that one can be absolutely open, say outrageous things if they are true. There is nothing to lose, for, as one accepts oneself, warts and all, in old age, others accept one . . . what might be questioned in a girl of twenty is applauded as "character," even enjoyed in a woman of seventy (Sarton, 1976, p. 27).

This woman's relationships include many people rather than only one person. In old age she views everything as opening out inside and around her. "The walls are dissolving between being and essence, and when they dissolve altogether, when our *selves*, as we have known them, dissolve into death, it will be that we have grown into another dimension" (Sarton, 1976, p. 27).

More and more women are living into their 80s. "There is much evidence to suggest that the eighties are an extraordinary period when the threads of a lifetime draw together into a skein of recognizable proportion, weighty with the wisdom of years" (Jones, 1978, p. 113). For some, the eighties are a period for taking stock and putting in order; for others, it is a time when their productivity becomes full. The experience of individuals in their 80s conveys the message that old age can be the crowning achievement of life.

The following life patterns of ordinary women in their 80s living in today's world illustrate the vitality that is possible:

Alice Pearce, 80, was elected Homecoming Queen last fall at Methodist College in Fayetteville, North Carolina. In addition to working for her degree in English at the college, where she is a junior, Pearce works part-time for the Fayetteville Symphony. . . . Her activities have given rise to the rumor that she has burned out two heart pacemakers (Jones, 1978 p. 115).

Henrietta Henius, 86, is a fragile-looking woman who appears never to have seen the harsher side of life. But for 33 years she was a social worker with the New York criminal courts, a kind of investigative reporter meeting and talking with all types of people. . . . Her hobby is locating missing heirs. She watches the *New York Times* listings of unclaimed bank accounts, then researches out-of-town telephone directories and other sources to track people down (Jones, 1978, p. 116).

[Grace] Petitclerc has worked for 50 years as an educational therapist, treating children with various sorts of learning disabilities. She maintains an active practice at 82. She took a master's degree in communications at the University of Hawaii at age 74. Now she is trying to cram a life's experience into a summary book she has titled *The New Child* (Jones, 1978, p. 119).

Lydia Torry, 86, lives by herself on a small island along the Canadian border near International Falls, Minnesota. During the winter she chips ice from the lake and hauls it to her house on a sled to melt into water. Her neighbors check in now and then, she says, bring her groceries periodically by boat or, when the lake is frozen, by snowmobile (Jones, 1978, p. 114).

LIFE PATTERNS

Role changes and the redirection of energies in older women's lives create a variety of life styles. Much of the classic research on life patterns is limited in its application to older women's lives today. The first two studies described below offer historical perspective and illustrate the need for further research focused on the life situations of women over 40.

Havighurst (1957) carried on one of the earliest studies describing women's lives after 40. In his investigations of the role performance of middle-aged people, he discovered two clusters of configurations; the roles in each cluster showed a high correlation with each other. One cluster contained the leisure, friend, citizen, and association member roles. This was labeled the "extra-family configuration." The "family configuration" consisted of the cluster of roles that included parent, spouse, and home-maker. The church member role had low correlation with other roles. The worker role had different patterns of correlation for women than for men; for women it was more closely related to the extra-family configuration.

Havighurst (1957) described most women's lives as simply structured because they were organized around the primary focus of home and family, while most men's lives had two foci, the job and the home. Women with family-centered patterns tended to be distributed fairly evenly over the 40-to-70 age range. Men could rate higher as a parent and homemaker with less effort than was expected of women. Thus, women employed outside the home met the social expectations of homemaker and parent less well than their male counterparts. However, the woman who worked success-fully at a job outside the home also tended to earn higher role-performance scores than men in the roles of citizen, friend, and user of leisure time.

Generally, there was no sharp decrease of role performance with age (Havighurst, 1957). Roles for women had a small increase as some entered the labor force in their middle years. Havighurst (1957) concluded that in the age range 40 to 70 "people's social competence remains on a plateau which has been achieved in early middle age and slopes very slightly downward toward the later years of life" (p. 341). In viewing social-class differences in role performance scores, generally the upper- and upper-middle-class people met the American expectations of performance better than people in lower classes. However, some lower-class people per-formed as well as the majority of upper-middle-class people.

Havighurst found 34 definable patterns or profiles of role performance. They were established in early middle age, i.e., in the 40s; 60-year-olds showed substantially the same patterns as 40-year-olds. Havighurst interpreted this cross-sectional data as evidence that patterns persist through middle age. Women's lives today as compared with those in 1957 may be less simply structured, with increasing numbers of older women entering the work force. The role cluster and persistence of patterns through middle age are quite applicable to, and important in, viewing the lives of older women today.

Additional support is offered as evidence of personality types remaining the same as women move from middle to old age. Six personality types emerged from Neugarten's (1964) ratings of 45 females. (The women in the study were white, ranged in age from 53 to 85 years, and lived in the metropolitan area of Kansas City.)

The *integrated women* had a balance between active strivings and passive-receptive qualities. "Although these women were maternal, they had evidently had long-standing identities more inclusive than the roles of wife and mother" (Neugarten, 1964, p. 177).

The *passive dependent* type represented women whose self-definition was structured around the roles of homemaker and mother. Their relatively good adjustment to aging rested on the availability of opportunities to continue their roles as homemaker, mother, and grandmother.

The *defended-constricted women* " . . . were uncomfortable with issues or impulses having to do with love, tenderness, or sexuality and protected themselves from anxiety by activity and outer-world involvement" (Neugarten, 1964, p. 179). They saw their activities as a search for a more complete feeling of fulfillment. Their satisfaction with life continued so long as they were able to keep their lives as active as possible and rigidly compartmentalized.

A fourth type, the *self-doubting women,* seemed to be in the midst of an identity crisis that was making them painfully aware that earlier emotional gratifications were no longer functional. There were signs of movement toward a new emotional equilibrium where they were able to be more self-assertive and to feel more competent.

The *competitive women* also seemed to be having an identity crisis. They were suffering from dissatisfaction, anger, and self-doubt; these feelings were precipitated by menopausal changes, children leaving home, and marital tensions. They were undertaking activities that "involved striving for competence and independence and sometimes hostile and competitive attitudes toward men, co-workers, and friends" (Neugarten, 1964, p. 182).

The *unintegrated women* did not sublimate their aggressive drives into behaviors that were flexible and empathetic. Their behavior seemed to show "a minimal control and an almost explosive reactivity" (Neugarten, 1964, p. 183).

The personality types were not, on the whole, related to age. Four of the six female types were distributed over wide age ranges, from the early 50s to the late 80s. (Six of the seven women in the "self-doubting" and "competitive" categories were in their early 50s.) Neugarten saw this finding of a lack of relationship between personality type and age as an implication that personalities maintain their characteristic patterns of organization as individuals move from middle to old age. There is a need to replicate this often-quoted study to determine if these six typologies still apply to the lives of older women.

Maas and Kuypers (1974) undertook a study on the lives of aging women and men who were not constrained by poverty. The subjects' average age was 70 years. They were economically well off and in above-average health. The 95 women all were mothers; at the time of the interviews, 62 of them were married, 28 were widows, and 5 were divorced or separated. The researchers found six life style clusters for the women: husband-centered wives, uncentered mothers, visiting mothers, work-centered mothers, disabled-disengaging mothers, and group-centered mothers.

The *husband-centered wives* had high involvement only as a marital partner. They did most things with their spouses. They did not see their children, grandchildren, or siblings often. Their focus was on home and neighborhood.

Eighty-one percent of the *uncentered mothers* were no longer married. In their daily lives interactions were not of an informal type, but were rather for occasions such as playing bridge or a spectator event. They visited their children and grandchildren more than the mothers in any other cluster, but only one-fourth were as highly involved as mothers. Fifty-seven percent were highly involved as grandmothers, but three other clusters had higher involvement in this area. Their way of life could be characterized as fundamentally receptive.

Although nearly all of the *visiting mothers* were married, marriage was not of central concern to them. They were highly involved in social interactions through visiting and being visited, parenting, and group membership. They had many recreational interests, many of which they pursued alone. "There is something traditionally village-like in the style of the . . . visiting mothers as they informally entertain visitors or busily go their rounds of family and groups of friends, all the while disapproving of what the world out there is becoming" (Maas and Kuypers, 1974, p. 57).

The *work-centered mothers* were highly involved as workers and very satisfied with their work situations. Nine of the 12 mothers were no longer married, but all had feelings of closeness with their children. They had many recreational interests and were very satisfied with their health.

The *disabled-disengaging mothers* were highly involved in the marital role but were not satisfied with their marriages. The sick role was an important dimension of their lives, as evidenced by recent visits to doctors for treatment and stays in the hospital within the past year. They had little interaction with friends, children, grandchildren, or groups within the community. Basically, there was nothing in life that the disabled-disengaging mother found very satisfying.

The *group-centered* mothers had high involvements as group members, citizens, and retirees. The home and informal interactions with friends were not important dimensions of these women's lives. None of their satisfactions was in the family area. They were somewhat dominant in their role as parent; marriage was not important. They were not highly involved with friends on an informal basis. "Rather, interaction in the formal organizations of clubs and frequent attendance at church mark the Gs [group-centered mothers] as more at home in structured or ritualized settings" (Maas and Kuypers, 1974, p. 74).

Thus, expanding interests and involvements beyond the family appear to increase the level of life satisfaction of wives and mothers in their later years if economic circumstances and health problems are not constricting influences. However, many older women live in poverty and therefore have limited opportunity for creating satisfying life styles.

The current realities of older women's lives can be separated into 13 role types (Jacobs, 1976). The *nurturers* "devote themselves to husband and kin as their primary or most salient activity, being grandmothers, mothers-in-law, housewives, etc." (Jacobs, 1976, p. 34). The *unemployed nurturers* no longer have a focus for their nurturing, while the *re-engaged nurturers* utilize their nurturing and other skills through paid and volunteer work or through remarriage.

The *chum networkers and/or leisureists* are a diverse group of women who gain their identity from passing time with other women in pursuit of pleasure and mutual support and affection. The *careerists* also find their primary satisfactions and important social relations with other women. However, the main identity comes from their work. The *retired careerists* may have at least as hard an adjustment to retirement as men.

Some *seekers* are motivated by a variety of reasons to experiment with fads, such as new religions and astrology. Other seekers are looking for job, educational, and volunteer opportunities. The *advocates* use their talents in the service of various causes—political, environmental, feminist, educational, and others. The *assertive seniors* direct their energies toward fighting for their collective rights.

The *faded beauties* fight the loss of youth with beauty salons, clothes, health clubs, and sometimes lovers. "Desperate for attention, *faded beauties* frequently resort to sickness for it, become the *doctorers*" (Jacobs, 1976, p. 38). The *doctorers* have a high rate of physician visits, hospitalization, and disability. Those who drink too much and succeed at suicide are labeled the *escapists*. Many began using alcohol late in life, possibly because of the stresses of growing old combined with loss of status and health. The *isolates* include women living alone who do not have enough money for necessities, let alone recreation or transportation, as well as women in institutions who receive only cursory care and few, if any, visitors.

Lowenthal and her associates (1975) studied men and women at four life stages; high school seniors, young newlyweds, middle-aged parents, and an older group about to retire. These middle- and lower-class subjects were interviewed for an average of 8 hours, with both open-ended material and structured research instruments. There were 27 middle-aged and 30 preretirement women in the study. The average age of the middle-aged women was 48 years; the older women, 58 years. Eighty-nine percent of the middle-aged women were married, compared with 73 percent of the preretirement women. More than a third of each group had some education beyond high school. Forty-eight percent of the middle-aged women were working full time; 4 percent, part time. Of the preretirement group, 53 percent of the women were working full time; 10 percent, part time.

The middle-aged women were almost exclusively family-centered. Employment did not appear to be a source of emotional satisfaction. They had few roles or activities outside of the family because their energies were consumed primarily with their children but also, to some extent, with their husbands. In describing their life styles, many "seemed in despair about their marriages and what they sensed to be an increasing dependency on their husbands" (Lowenthal, Thurnher, and Chiriboga, 1975, p. 219). Their hopes focused on their children. Of all the women in the sample, they were the least cheerful about whatever they saw to be their main transition, and only half had a positive attitude toward whatever that transition might be. Women who considered their husband's retirement in the distant future as their main transition were more pessimistic than those women who viewed their youngest child's leaving home as their main transition.

Half of the women in the preretirement stage anticipated their own retirement from paid jobs as their main transition; the other half emphasized their husbands' retirement. The preretirement women had a more optimistic outlook toward the next five years than the middle-aged women, though not necessarily toward the retirement stage in particular. Fourteen percent of the preretirement women were completely negative in their attitude toward their main transition; these were primarily widowed, divorced, and single women. Most preretirement women retained the family-centeredness and gained no real satisfaction from their jobs. They did have a stronger interest in personal growth and socially oriented goals than the middle-aged women. However, their main goals centered on perpetuating a comfortable and familiar life style.

Planning was almost nonexistent, except in the preretirement stage. Even those who did have plans were more likely to be thinking of a trip rather than preparing for a new way of life. The few women at the "empty nest" transition who had plans focused on plans for their children. Their plans for their own use of time were vague and diffuse. Among preretirement women, the unattached working women saw their retirement as a crucial transition and felt the need for planning. Preretirement women who pictured their spouses' retirement as their main transition let their future be determined by fate or by their husbands.

SOCIAL NETWORKS

Social interactions are frequently an important element in older women's life situations. The beneficial aspects of a high level of involvement in social networks of various types has been demonstrated in numerous research studies. Extensive social activity with age peers can be an effective alternative for the marital or occupational role (Blau, 1973). Among the retired and widowed, high morale was associated with high participation scores. Low morale was typical among retired people (69 percent) who had low participation scores. The morale of the widowed and retirees with extensive social activity was similar to that of both married persons and employed people.

Relationships with children are not an effective substitute for social interactions with spouses and coworkers, in Blau's view. "Indeed because friendship rests on mutual choice and mutual need and involves a voluntary exchange of sociability between equals, it sustains a person's sense of usefulness and self-esteem more effectively than filial relationships" (Blau, 1973, p. 67). In our rapidly changing society, Blau sees a gulf between the generations; this creates a need for older women and men to associate with their own generation in order to have higher morale.

Voluntary associations are often seen as a means of continuing the involvement of older people in social networks outside of the family. In reviewing research in this area, Lowenthal and Robinson (1976) found that, with the exception of church membership, the majority of persons do not belong to such groups. Of those who do, most only belong to one organization.

Membership, however, does not necessarily mean involvement. Women are more likely than men to continue to attend church regularly and to participate in other religious activities. Older people who are still working, married, and entertaining friends occasionally are more likely to be involved in voluntary associations. "To summarize the majority of studies, it appears, as with other leisure patterns, that direct participation in volunteer associations in old age depends to a considerable extent on styles established earlier in life" (Lowenthal and Robinson, 1976, p. 445).

The value of social relationships for the elderly has produced a new kind of service: centers for senior citizens. Taietz (1976) interviewed a total of 920 older men and women in 32 communities in New York State. Three-fourths of the membership of the senior centers were females. Sixty-three percent of the women were widowed, 31 percent separated or divorced, and 9 percent had never married. The income of the female members was lower than that of the males; 49 percent had annual incomes of less than $2,000. Taietz found that older people who were active in organizations and had a strong attachment to the community tended to be members of a senior center. The senior centers he surveyed did not attract isolated older women and men.

Volunteering is particularly important for older women. Programs drawing on the services of older volunteers, as well as senior centers, have been established on the assumption that these volunteer organizations can reduce social isolation among older adults. The talents of the older volunteer are receiving national attention as many agencies or organizations incorporate volunteer positions for older people into their formal structure. In a literature review on volunteering, Payne and Whittington (1976) reported that older volunteers were overwhelmingly female and widowed (60 to 80 percent).

One source of social activity and volunteer opportunities is programs providing meals for older persons in group settings in the community. These programs were developed nationwide to serve healthful meals, to teach older people more about nutrition, and to offer social, recreational, educational activities (*Meals*, 1972). Volunteers help find participants, act as hosts and hostesses, keep conversation rolling, and help serve the food. These group meals help to relieve the loneliness and inactivity in the lives of older women and men.

The Meals on Wheels program has become well-known in its efforts to bring nutritional food to home-bound persons (Smith, 1973). Volunteers are often a central component of the program. In addition to making deliveries, they may stay to visit during the meal. Volunteers can also report other needs the home-bound person may have.

The Foster Grandparent Program, initiated by the Administration on Aging, is one of the most successful projects providing opportunities for service (Smith, 1973). The volunteers, who must be over 60 and have a lower level of income, are paid a minimum wage. They work with children in institutions, including those for retarded and disturbed children, convalescent hospitals, and temporary care centers. The mental and physical health of both the older people and the children frequently improves in the atmosphere of concern and individual attention.

In addition to providing social contact, volunteer jobs can help women use present skills and develop new ones. They also offer an alternative way to gain useful work experience when paid jobs are not available, and may provide contacts for entry-level paid positions (Hybels and Mueller, 1978).

For the volunteering role to remain attractive over an extended period of time, the older woman needs to feel that the volunteering offers her status and self-fulfillment (Payne and Whittington, 1976). "[Volunteers] must be given sufficient time to explore task options, to seek work which captures their interest and meets their time and energy requirements, and, above all, to sense accepting attitudes among the paid staff, before they give their full commitment to volunteer work" (*Releasing*, 1976, p. 57).

Organizations providing volunteer and social activities can be encouraged to include older women in the decision-making processes. Older women would have a status normally associated with that deriving from paid work, and direct input concerning their needs, interests, and skills. For example, senior centers often offer gardening, needlecraft, and other classes of a stereotypically feminine focus. The inclusion of older women in program decisions can lead to a wider variety of activities, and also encourage the development of new and more satisfying interests by older women.

FRIENDSHIP PATTERNS

Participation in a friendship group becomes more important after 70, when other group memberships, such as work groups and voluntary organizations, are the exception. "The stability of the *network* of relationships within a group of friends or co-workers prevents mutual awareness of the gradual alterations taking place among the participants, particularly, if these changes do not interfere with a person's ability to share in the group's activities" (Blau, 1973, p. 108). Thus, older people who belonged to a "friendship clique" considered themselves old less often than those who were not a part of such a group.

In their study of transitions at different points in the life span, Lowenthal and her associates (1975) concluded that friendship patterns do not remain the same. The middle-aged women and men had fewer friends than older persons about to retire. The energies and emotions of the middle-aged people were focused elsewhere. The middle-aged women were quite simplistic in their perceptions of the important qualities of friendship; for example, one middle-aged woman mentioned only one dimension, that of similar interests, as important in her friends. In contrast, an older woman about to retire used twelve dimensions to describe her friends. "In fact, the overwhelming majority of people at this later life stage have highly complex or multidimensional friendships" (Lowenthal, Thurnher, and Chiriboga, 1975, p. 61).

Research tells us a few things about the number, intensity, and complexity of social contacts as determined by the age and sex of individuals. Friendships are more extensive for older women than for older men (Powers and Bultena, 1976). Older women more often turn to friends, usually other women of nearly the same age, for intimacy and affection, while older men find support from their wives. In a national survey, Harris (1975) asked people 65 and over to whom they felt close enough to talk about things that really bothered them. Thirty-nine percent of the women mentioned spouses. Women over age 65 are more likely to be widowed and so would not have spouses to mention. However, even older married women were more likely than men to mention friends, relatives, or children as their confidants rather than spouses (Lowenthal and Haven, 1968).

There are sex, marital, age, and socioeconomic status differences involved in the intimate relationships of people 60 years and older (Lowenthal and Haven, 1968). "Women are more likely than men to have an intimate relationship at all age levels (from 60 years on), and the differences between sexes are especially pronounced in those under 65, where nearly three-fourths of the women and only half of the men reported they had a confidant" (Lowenthal and Haven, 1968, p. 398). Married women were most likely to have confidants (81 percent), as compared with single (67 percent) and widowed (65 percent) women. Women with a high socioeconomic status had a larger pool of social resources and were considerably more likely to have confidants than those with a low status (77 percent as compared with 56 percent).

Intimate relationships may serve as a buffer against the loss of role or the reduction of other more formal social interactions. Lowenthal and Haven (1968) found that social interactions and roles could be decreased without affecting morale if the individual had a confidant. The confidant helps morale even during the dramatic role losses of widowhood and retirement. "An individual who has been widowed within seven years, and who has a confidant, has even higher morale than a person who remains married but lacks a confidant. The retired with a confidant rank the same in regard to morale as those still working who have no confidant. . . ." (Lowenthal and Haven, 1968, p. 397).

Older women are reported to distribute their social contacts among a number of people: friends, neighbors, children and their families, spouses, siblings, intimate friends, and other relatives (Powers and Bultena, 1976). Women develop and sustain close relationships and maintain a greater diversity in all forms of social contact than do older men. Older women may have the adaptability for survival in late life because of the quality of social interaction that older men lack (Lowenthal and Haven, 1968; Powers and Bultena, 1976).

LIVING ARRANGEMENTS

The family today is an interdependent unit in which one or more members must undertake activities outside the home. The present-day family has two primary functions: procreation and socialization of offspring (Karcher and Linden, 1974). The nuclear family with husband and wife present and competent can perform these functions adequately. Neither older men nor women have a recognized role to play within this nuclear family structure. When an older person is incorporated into the present-day family, conflict can be created by competition for existing family roles.

The American Geriatric Society reports that "more and more older people are living alone as widowed or single adults or with unrelated peers, rather than with their children or in institutions" (Alvarez, 1972, p. 77). Two out of five women 75 and over live alone, as compared to one out of six for ages 55 to 64 years (U.S. Department of Commerce, 1976b, p. 47).

It is predicted that there will continue to be an increase in older persons who live alone (Alvarez, 1972). The tendency toward smaller family sizes means families are more likely to live in smaller housing units that do not have room for a member of the third generation. Women, increasingly in the work force, will not be available to stay home caring for aging parents.

The age span between generations has decreased, and increasing numbers of people, especially women, are living into their 80s and 90s. More frequently adult children are coping with their own aging problems, such as adjusting to retirement and less income, at the same time that their parents are facing increased limitations (Gelfand, Olsen, and Block, 1978). The children's capacity to offer shared living arrangements may be lessened.

Another factor that affects the living situations of older people is the more selective admission policies of mental hospitals. Mental hospitals are no longer places for people who are physically infirm or frail and lack someone to care for them. Some of those who are refused have no choice but to return to their homes to live alone without adequate care and contact with the outside world.

The location of her home and the type of living situation may have a significant effect on the extent of the older woman's social contacts. Rosow (1968) studied 1,200 middle-class and working-class residents of several hundred Cleveland apartment buildings. The men were 65 or older, the women 62 or older. He found that the number of older people's local friends did vary with the proportion of older neighbors and that these friends were basically drawn from older neighbors of same sex, marital status, and social class.

In areas of increased density of neighbors that were same sex and age, women's social activity increased more than that of the men. The middle-class single and widowed people were "extremely sensitive to density differences" (Rosow, 1968, p. 385). Working-class women, whether married or not, responded in identical fashion to differences in density. "Their basic local orientation is so strong that density alone accounts for differences in their neighboring" (Rosow, 1968, p. 385). People over 75 had significantly more local contacts than those under 75. The neighboring of self-supporting women was not affected by density while they were working. However, after they retired, "the proportion with high local contact increased progressively with density from 21 percent of those in Normal areas to 58 percent of those in the Dense" (Rosow, 1968, p. 386).

Twenty-two percent of people 65 and over live in small towns or on farms and have an income that is $400 to $700 less than similar older people in metropolitan areas (Carp, 1976). The rural aged are especially affected by the scarcity of younger family members to assist them, but there is evidence that small towns provide a favorable social setting for the later years. With greater awareness of the elderly in their midst, smaller communities may need to offer financial assistance and aid in the tasks of daily living.

Change of residence because of deteriorating neighborhood conditions, decreased income, and urban renewal may have adverse effects on the social networks of older women. Brand and Smith (1974) found that females 65 and over who were forced to relocate to unfamiliar areas because of urban renewal had significantly lower life satisfaction than those who remained in familiar surroundings. Interrupted relationships with old friends caused by the relocation increased feelings of isolation and loneliness. "Compared to the nonrelocated group, relocated subjects were generally less active and had fewer social contacts" (Brand and Smith, 1974, p. 340).

Physical, mental, or financial decrements may put severe restrictions on the mobility of older people. They may be dependent on public transportation, though even this mode of travel may be out of the question because of illness, fear, or disability. They may lack family and friends to call on, or be too proud to ask for favors that they cannot reciprocate. Thus, the immediate neighborhood assumes as much importance as an older person's living quarters. Clark and Anderson (1967) see a phenomenon of the "geriatric ghetto" as fast becoming a common landmark in American cities. "These little pockets of elderly residents usually spring up on the fringes of downtown commercial districts where—because the redevelopment bulldozers have not yet arrived—rents are cheap and shops handy" (p. 34).

Communal Living Arrangements

Hochschild (1973) described a communal life style that developed in Merrill Court, a small apartment building in San Francisco. Thirty-seven of the 43 residents were women, mainly widows. They ranged in age from the 60s to over 80. They first began gathering around a new coffee machine in the recreation room. Six months later there were many activities, such as bowling, classes on various subjects, birthday parties, and visits to nearby nursing homes. Most residents belonged to the Merrill Court Service Club, which set up committees and chairpersons for various activities.

There was also "an informal network of friendships that formed over a cup of coffee in the upstairs apartments" (Hochschild, 1973, p. 51). Most floor neighbors became friends; friendships were mainly confined to people living on the same floor. This neighboring was a way of relaying information or misinformation about others, and also a way to detect sickness. The habits of neighbors were known, so anything unusual was immediately spotted. The widows who were in good health took it on themselves to care for others in poor health.

"There were rivalries and differences in Merrill Court but neither alienation nor isolation. More obvious were the many small, quiet favors, keeping an eye out for a friend and sharing a good laugh" (Hochschild, 1973, p. 54). Hochschild describes most of the residents as "social siblings." They were equals among themselves: they wanted and could give basically the same things. When they exchanged services, it was usually the same kinds of services they themselves could perform. Two neighbors might exchange corn bread and jam, although each knew how to make both corn bread and jam. The exchange process reinforced a friendship relationship.

Hochschild (1973) saw autonomy as a central factor in the development of the sibling bond. Institutions such as nursing homes and convalescent hospitals foster nonreciprocal relationships to the attendants and nurses, in Hochschild's view. The residents cannot meet as independent equals. The widows of Merrill Court took care of themselves and others and were part of an age stratum with which they shared similar wants, abilities, rewards, and failings.

Institutionalization

Although the public may think that old people are all in nursing homes, the fact is that they are not. Only 4 percent of the population over 65 are in institutions. Of this number, the overwhelming majority are women. "About 62 percent of the institutionalized are women and 38 percent are men" (Brody, 1970, p. 286). Since older women outnumber older men in increasing proportion with age, it is not surprising that a higher proportion of women require institutional care. Some types of institutions providing care for older people are nursing homes, county homes, psychiatric hospitals, general hospitals, voluntary homes for the aged, and facilities for long-term chronic illness.

What situations result in institutionalization for an older woman? Other members of the household may be ill or infirm and unable to provide care. The home may become overcrowded when a new baby arrives, and grandma has to give up the spare room. An older woman may actually lose a place to live because another family member is hospitalized, the family moves and cannot or will not take her, or the family is evicted. Strain placed on the family members because of the illness or infirmity of the older woman may create difficulties in the living situation. Friction with another member of the household, usually an in-law, is a common reason for the displacement of an older woman. Or the woman may have outlived other family members, the home is broken up, and an institution is the final solution.

Older people are very concerned about their chances of being institutionalized. Palmore (1976) studied normal aged people over a 20-year period in the first attempt to provide a general estimate. He concluded that the total chance of institutionalization before death among people living in the community would be about one in four.

People living alone, never married, separated from spouses, and those with no living children or with only one or two children were the categories with higher rates of institutionalization (Palmore, 1976). Women have a higher rate than men mainly because they more often fall into the categories just mentioned.

Being forced by circumstances to turn to others for care and surrendering the direction of one's personal life are two of the situations that most negatively affect the mental health of older persons in institutions (Brody, 1970). Elderly institutionalized females perceived themselves as having fewer choices in their lives than older women living in the community (Hulicka, Morganti, and Cataldo, 1975). Self-directed activities are often reduced because of particular institutional regulations, limits on the amount of personal possessions, and the dependency that is encouraged by institutional living (Abdo et al., 1973). Institutions are beginning to recognize that staff and other arrangements can be organized to promote a view of each person as an autonomous individual who should have as much control over personal activities, possessions, and life decisions as possible.

Provision for life-enhancing services needs to be a central component in an institution's program. Providing coffee and orange juice in the recreation room during the hour before breakfast increased the social interactions of handicapped older women, aged 68 to 90 years (Blackman, Howe, and Pinkston, 1976). The simple activity of making instant pudding as a group provided an opportunity to awaken the dulled senses of disoriented older women and increased their awareness of each other (Derx, 1972). Institutionalized females who received a weekly facial, a morning application of cosmetics, and an evening cleansing of the skin showed a significant increase in self-esteem as compared with females in the same situation who were visited regularly by a number of volunteers (Ernst, 1974). Group activity programs for apathetic older adults can result in new interest of the residents in personal grooming, conversational interaction, initiating their own activities, and desire to work (Brody, 1970). Encouragement of continuing family relationships is a key factor in fostering good mental health of those institutionalized.

"About 80 percent of older persons in institutionalized homes are in commercial nursing homes, and this represents almost a million people" (Butler, 1975, p. 263). The possibilities for exploitation in institutional settings are numerous. For example, nursing homes do not provide comprehensive medical care. Care must be obtained from family physicians or private physicians assigned by a welfare agency or the home itself. A doctor may quickly visit a large number of residents in one day and then submit a substantial bill (Butler, 1975). People needing institutionalized care are very much at the mercy of those who provide care. Governmental action is badly needed to provide fundamental reforms directed toward humane and innovative care. Since so many residents in these institutions are older women, this issue is of special concern to all women.

A large proportion of the present nursing home population does not need the services that are supposed to be available there (Karcher and Linden, 1974). Nursing homes are serving as a repository for many healthy aged women who are displaced from a family setting. These women need care structures designed to meet their needs without the stigma that is attached to personal care or "old-age" homes.

Congregate care facilities offer living arrangements for those older women who can no longer live in a completely independent manner in the community, yet do not need the total care of an institution. A wide range of intermediate facilities exist and are evolving. "The most visible are apartment buildings, hotels, and retirement villages for the elderly which have increased rapidly in the past ten years" (Brody, 1970, pp. 307–308). These may provide only shelter, or one or more additional services, such as medical care, meals, housekeeping, shopping, or recreation. Boarding homes and foster homes for the elderly are also facilities that are increasing in number. Only a broad spectrum of congregate facilities will meet the needs of the heterogeneous aging population.

Weinfeld Group Living Residence is a renovated townhouse complex in Evanston, Illinois, which opened four years ago as an experiment in congregate housing for 11 older women and 1 older man. Each unit, shared by two women, has two bedrooms, a bathroom, living room, a kitchen, and a door to the outside. Meals are provided in a central dining room where residents set the table and wash the dishes afterwards. Counseling, health care, homemaking aid, and activities are available. The aim at Weinfeld is to encourage residents to maintain ties with the community and with their families while providing only as much help as is needed. The 11 women, whose average age is 82, and the 1 man could not live independently in the community. "Now pooling what strengths age permits, they give each other emotional and physical sustenances in an environment that feels and smells more or less the way home once did" (Wax, 1976, p. 38).

The provision of services can make a significant contribution to the older woman's ability to continue living in the community. Women who received home aide service had significantly fewer days of institutionalization than those who did not (Nielson et al., 1972). The home aides helped the older women carry out tasks they were unable to do themselves or ones that a family member might have to do for them. In addition to the home aide service, the presence of a family member or friend in the household able to handle evening or overnight care, reduced the chances of institutionalization to the extent that it would happen by chance only once in a hundred similar situations.

Halfway Houses and Shared Homes

Halfway houses provide community-based residences; usually, the house is located in an urban or suburban area where the residents can take advantage of community services. The length of residency depends on the type of clientele and the nature of their problems (Streib and Haug, 1978). Wife abuse centers are an example of halfway houses for women. One such center in Florida plans to expand its services to include displaced homemakers and other older women in distress.

Sharing a home with other persons can be a practical form of living arrangement. The Share-A-Home Association, Inc., a nonprofit organization chartered under Florida law, provides information and assistance, such as loans and furnishings, to persons forming a "family" (Streib and Haug, 1978). The family consists of nonrelated older adults who share a house and the expense of running it. A paid staff takes care of finances, housekeeping, food, laundry, and other services. "The Share-A-Home concept meets three important social-psychological needs which have been stressed for many persons: (1) free choice; (2) association with others who give affection and concern; and (3) feelings of dignity and autonomy" (Streib and Haug, 1978, p. 290).

Retirement Communities

"If the present proportion of retired persons in the 65 and over age bracket continues, two decades hence there should be about 8 million men and 14 million women living in retirement" (Gersuny, 1970, p. 282). A new and growing housing trend is the development of retirement communities. These communities have been criticized as a means of putting older people out of sight and as "hedonistic in spirit and devoted only to pleasure, recreation, and leisure activities" (Streib, 1976, p. 172). In a positive light, retirement communities can be seen as a status buffer. "They provide a protective environment which tends to shield the older persons from the acknowledgement of downward mobility or a loss of status" (Streib, 1976, p. 172). Streib described the residents of these communities as mainly affluent middle-class or upper-middle-class people whose previous life style provided opportunity for considerable time devoted to leisure, friendship, and recreation.

Gersuny (1970) explored the rhetoric of the retirement home industry. Brochures of retirement homes invariably develop the theme that one never need be lonely again; they promise friendship with congenial people. "We will introduce you personally to new men and women friends for a brim-ful life." Rossmoor Leisure World, located in California, Maryland, and New Jersey, makes available vacation resort facilities: swimming, golfing, riding, and hobby shops. It advertises more than housing—the advantages of total community living (Butler, 1975).

Opportunities for socializing in a retirement community of 400 residents were studied by Seguin (1973). The median age of the residents was 80 years. Women were a significant proportion of the residents, outnumbering the men six to one. It was estimated that seven in eight residents had taken specific responsibility in the Garden Club, a voluntary association of all residents. Residents also had opportunities for involvement in the resident organization that controlled the community. Informal social networks appeared to be extensive and important for many of the residents. Creation of a resident social structure and the development of linkages with the wider organizational structure of the retirement community were important aspects in providing for the socialization of the residents.

Most older women living in retirement communities are there because their husband's assets allow such a life style. A major portion of American women today cannot afford such living arrangements. Longitudinal research concerning older people in a variety of living situations is needed (Carp, 1976).

> The years of "aging" are long and now comprise a significant portion of life span. The person is far different during his final year of life than in the first after he reached the chronological age, retirement, or other status which defined him as "old." The life-space must be made flexible and sensitive to the changing needs of its participants (Carp, 1976, p. 264).

MAJOR CONCERNS OF OLDER PEOPLE

The major concerns of older people who wrote to the syndicated newspaper columnist "Dear Abby" were loneliness, interpersonal problems with a spouse and other relatives, sexual problems, and rejection (Gaitz and Scott, 1975). The writers were predominantly women (66 percent). More women than men were concerned with illness, rejection, problems with spouses and relatives, and etiquette and grooming; more men than women wrote of sexual problems and problems of finding a new mate. "The older writers often express succinctly the awareness of their limitations (physical, economic, losses of friends and family) and at the same time indicate a strong desire to manage their lives with minimum assistance in spite of these limitations" (Gaitz and Scott, 1975, p. 49).

A national poll by Harris (1975) revealed some sex differences affecting the degree to which people 65 and older suffer from various problems.

Older women tended to report fear of crime as a very serious problem. Loneliness seemed to afflict older women somewhat more seriously than it did older men. Older men were slightly more likely to complain of not enough job opportunities than older women, but the differences were minimal. "All in all, the key demographics such as income, race, sex and education are more important indicators of serious problems than age" (Harris, 1975).

Warren (1974) surveyed 56 females and 9 males living in low-income urban housing to determine their self-perceptions of independence. The respondents ranged in age from 60 to 90 years old; 45 of the 56 were widowed; 74 percent lived alone. A checklist of questions asked about six tasks: (1) bathing and grooming, (2) dressing, (3) meal preparation, (4) laundry, (5) housecleaning, and (6) getting out and around. Twenty-seven, or 41.5 percent, of the subjects considered themselves completely independent; the remaining 38, or 58.5 percent, reported some limitations within the six tasks.

Subjects were also asked what tasks concerned them most in managing on their own. Only 37 percent expressed any concerns. Those who did were about evenly divided between concern over their ability to get out and around and worry over being able to continue housecleaning activities. The fact that there were 58.5 percent who had reported some degree of dependency on the tasks described above led Warren (1974) to suggest that "many who had reported no concerns had adapted to their limitations, had developed an attitude of resignation, or a seeming indifference that masked their real concerns from the casual observer" (p. 335).

SOCIAL CHANGE

Many disruptions are possible in older women's lives. Research generally has been focused on the means by which individual women cope with their environment rather than on the social environments. Changes in cultural structures could provide more support during transitions in this period in life.

An overall view of the life situations of older women indicates that several of the more satisfying patterns are dependent on the presence of family, a job, an organization, or friends. An affiliative family form is a structure that would integrate members of the older population into society and into the family system by creating occupational and family roles for them. This structure is described as "any combination of husband/father, wife/mother, and their children, plus one or more older persons, recognized as part of the kin network and called by a designated kin term" (Claven and Vatter, 1972, p. 409). The family members may or may not live in one household. Monetary remuneration may or may not be involved. The basic ingredient is voluntary commitment to one another in the affiliative family unit. Older women in the affiliative family form could help with the socialization of the child and the emotional support of family members within the home setting. They could staff services for low-income families. Thus, they could regain homemaking, and perhaps working, roles. Allowing women continued access to jobs or careers would provide significant roles for some older women (Bart, 1969).

Lowenthal and her associates (1975) concluded from their findings that the potential of older women was being wasted. They suggested short-term changes: well-advertised educational programs for all middle-aged and older people, including minorities and the poor; training facilities to provide career-change opportunities; industry and media campaigns to combat the youth orientation in our society; and preventive mental health programs. Ultimately, however, the social institutions must change so that older people are integrated within the vital institutions.

> What is needed is a life-course orientation in all of our social, educational, and economic institutions, one which will have its impact on adolescents and young adults so that, when they approach the twenty- or thirty-year postparental stage, they will not be forced to project as empty a future as do most people who now make up the postparental and retirement cohorts (Lowenthal, Thurnher, and Chiriboga, 1975, p. 244).

Six major needs were perceived in the older adults studied by Clark and Anderson (1967):

> Satisfaction of these needs are components of the "Good Life":
> 1. Sufficient autonomy to permit continued integrity of the self;
> 2. Agreeable relationships with other people, some of whom are willing to provide help when needed without losing respect for the recipient;
> 3. A reasonable amount of personal comfort in body, mind, and physical environment;
> 4. Stimulation of the mind and imagination in ways that are not overtaxing of physical strength;
> 5. Sufficient movement to permit variety in the surroundings;

6. Some degree of passionate involvement with life, to escape preoccupation with death (Clark and Anderson, 1967, pp. 232–233).

The life situations of many older women incorporate a few of the above components. The concerns of older women have been neglected until recently. "Solution to problems of neglect cannot be found by changing old people, but require changes in society" (Lozier, 1975, p. 297). Societal changes that provide support for a view of life after 40 as a time of redirection of energies and redefinition of roles rather than a period of role loss and dependency are essential.

SUMMARY

This chapter has described various aspects of the life situations of women over forty in American society. Women today have several decades of living after their mothering role is over. They may choose to focus more on themselves and less on responsibility toward others. The dimensions of a woman's life are formed by factors such as family involvement, employment, friendships and activities, health, and the personality of the individual woman. Her life pattern is created by the interaction of the various aspects of her life.

Involvement in a network of social contacts can be a very beneficial aspect of older women's life situations. Voluntary associations can provide contacts with people outside the family. Volunteering is often an important experience in the lives of older women.

Friendship patterns appear to change over time, and the number of friendships vary, as do the perceptions women have of their friends. Middle-aged women tend to have less energy and emotion to devote to the development of friendships than women approaching the retirement stage of life. As women age, they appear to distribute their social contacts over a wider variety of people than do older men. They are also more likely to have a confidant than are older men. The diversity and intimacy dimensions may contribute to women's greater adaptability for survival in later life.

More older women are living alone or with friends than in the past. Smaller family homes, more women employed, and adult children's own aging problems are some of the factors that decrease the possibility of older women living with family members. Physical limitations, a decrease in finances, and poor mental health conditions can all negatively affect living arrangements and social contacts in the community. Retirement communities, communal living arrangements, housing with some services provided, and nursing homes are living arrangements that offer varying degrees of independence to older women.

Limitations created by physical changes, illness, financial resources, and loss of friends and family members may be important concerns of older women, depending on individual situations. Often coupled with an awareness of these limitations is a strong desire to maintain as much independence within daily living as possible. Two ways that older women may adapt to limitations are through seeking assistance as needed or by developing an attitude of resignation or indifference that hides real concerns about loss and dependency.

The institutions of our society need to offer older women more opportunities to continue employment, education, and leisure activities. More support is needed to maintain adequate living conditions, good physical and mental health, and contacts with friends and family. Rather than expecting women to cope with loss and change using only the individual resources they possess, institutions should provide financial, emotional, and social supports. These supports would enable more women to direct their energies toward new goals leading to more satisfying life situations.

■6
Family Relations

Factors such as children leaving home, separation and divorce, aging parents, and the husband's death cause changes in the family relationships of older women. For example, the older woman must make adjustments in her mothering role after her children have left home. The first section of this chapter will focus on the period after the youngest child has left home—the postparental period. Marriage satisfaction in later life, displaced homemakers, divorce, and widowhood are discussed in the next sections. Remarriage, the changing role of the grandmother and the relationships between parents and adult children are the subjects of the final three sections.

The life cycle of women has changed dramatically over the last 80 years. In 1890 the average woman was widowed before her last child left home; her last child would marry when she was 55; and she would live to about age 68 (Neugarten and Datan, 1973). In 1966 a woman in her middle to late 30s could expect her last child to marry when she was 48; her husband to die when she was 64; and she could expect to live to age 74 or beyond. Today a woman who reaches 65 years of age can expect to live 18 more years on the average, or until the age of 83. Thus, the life span of women now may extend more than 30 years beyond the time when the youngest child leaves home.

POSTPARENTAL PERIOD

Due to their involvement in homemaking and child-rearing as primary roles, most women experience changes in family roles earlier than men. For a mother, the period after her children leave home may be a time of finding new ways of nurturing, a time of freedom and new goals, or a time of emptiness that she cannot easily fill. In a study of sex roles and depression, Pearlin (1975) found a negative relationship between age and disenchantment with the homemaking role. Older women were less distressed at spending their time exclusively at homemaking tasks than younger women because they had expected to spend their lives in this role. They have tended to operate within a more traditional set of values, and their homemaking role became easier as the children grew older and left home.

More and more women are responding to the postparental period by returning to the labor force, usually to clerical and sales jobs that require little training or skill. Increasingly, educated middle-class women are gaining further formal education so that they can qualify for more challenging work. However, the lack of resources and experience are obstacles that keep many women from creating new and satisfying roles when their earlier ones no longer exist (Blau, 1973). The relationship of employment to the psychological adjustment of older mothers was studied by Powell (1977). These college-educated women were married and in their late 50s at the time of the study. Significantly higher psychiatric symptom scores were exhibited by women not employed outside the home than by women employed full-time. In contrast, family-oriented women in Lowenthal's (1975) study were depressed and anxious even though a majority worked outside the home. Possibly the satisfactions from outside employment did not have the emotional significance to these women that they received from the mothering role (Higgins, 1975).

Women who have a strong family orientation are clearly in a more critical period after their children grow up and leave home than men at a similar point (Lowenthal, Thurnher, and Chiriboga, 1975). The passage through the postparental transition involves more than the youngest child's graduating from high school and establishing himself or herself in the world (Spence and Lonner, 1971). The complexity of the transition is demonstrated by the expectations women may hold for their children and the effect these expectations may have on their expectations for their own life course.

It was as important for their offspring to be "on time" as it was to be "on time" themselves. This notion becomes critical when it can be demonstrated that the children's failure to progress as expected will delay or threaten the smooth unfolding of the mother's later life expectations (Spence and Lonner, 1971, p. 373).

For example, a daughter's refusal or failure to marry right after finishing her education may interfere with a mother's expectations of her role as a grandmother. In addition, women who expressed fears about their children's ability to lead a successful life did not feel free to pursue new goals for themselves. "Thus, when they spoke of alternative goals toward which they could restructure their lives, they sounded very tentative, vague, and even pessimistic" (Spence and Lonner, 1971, p. 373).

Moving out of the mothering role may allow a woman more choice in whether or not she conforms to traditional female sex roles. Between the ages of 40 and 50, the personality development of older women who have led traditional lives may follow at least two different patterns. According to Livson (1976), the key factor in the different patterns of development was the fit between a woman's life style and her personality. Some women who were not motivated to change themselves or their situations appeared happy with their life styles. Even after their children left home, these women continued to feel of value in the role of wife and mother and to find satisfaction in their relationships with others outside the family. Consequently, there was a minimal conflict between their personalities and their life styles.

Another group of women appeared to have an identity crisis when their children reached adolescence. "Having suppressed their intellectual competence and grown away from child-care skills, they seem unable for a time to connect with a workable identity" (Livson, 1976, p. 113). Their children leaving home stimulated them to revive their intellectual skills and originality as part of their identities and to become more goal oriented.

Several conditioning situations provide an opportunity to anticipate postparental roles (Deutscher, 1968). Life in the urban high school can move the children into a world foreign to the parents. Children depart for college or service in the armed forces and return periodically. The small group of postparental spouses interviewed by Deutscher appeared to have opportunities to prepare for postparental life, and most took advantage of these opportunities.

Married couples in the postparental phase of life may see this period as a time of freedom: freedom from the economic responsibility of children, freedom to be mobile, freedom from housework and other chores. "No longer do the parents need to live the selfconsciously restricted existence of models for their own children . . ." (Deutscher, 1968, p. 264). The positive effect on the marriage as a result of the children's leaving may be the balancing factor that keeps happiness from declining during the postparental period (Glenn, 1975). Postparental women report distinctly greater marital happiness on the whole than women in the same age range who are still in the parental role.

Thus, the myth that the period when children leave home is usually a time of crisis for women is challenged by research findings. Reactions depend on individual differences and life situations. Younger women are having fewer children, and more are working during child-rearing years. Thus, many will be younger when their children leave home, and their work roles more frequently will be already established. Entering the postparental period is likely to be less of a traumatic transition period for many older women of the future.

MARRIAGE

Does marriage become more or less satisfying to the older woman as the years pass? Studies of marital satisfaction over the family life cycle show two patterns. One group of studies suggests a continual decline in satisfaction, while other research data show a leveling off of satisfaction, followed by an increase in satisfaction in the later stages of marriage (Spanier, Lewis, and Cole, 1975). For example, in studying couples who have been married up to 20 years, Pineo (1968) found a number of changes that indicated disenchantment in the later years of marriage. There was a general drop of marital satisfaction and adjustment. Frequency of sexual intercourse diminished, and the amount of shared activity dropped. "Confiding, kissing, and reciprocal settlement of disagreements become less frequent; more individuals report loneliness" (Pineo, 1968, p. 258). In a counter example, retired working class couples reported little or no change in their marital relationship on retirement and felt a high degree of marital satisfaction (Dressler, 1973).

Role strain may be the critical variable in determining marital satisfaction at a particular stage of the family life cycle (Rollins and Cannon, 1974). Various research studies have demonstrated that the number and intensity of social roles begin to decrease in the middle years. Burr (1970) obtained data from a random sample of 116 middle-aged couples about their degree of satisfaction over six areas of marital interaction: (1) handling of finances, (2) social activities, (3) tasks, (4) companionship, (5) sex, and (6) children. The findings showed the school-age stage (oldest child between 6 and 12 years) to be the most difficult. For women, there was an increase in satisfaction in all six areas after this stage. Thus, viewing marriage and family in terms of role strain means that role strain would be the least and marital satisfaction the greatest at both ends of the family cycle.

A number of factors other than life cycle stage affect the marital satisfaction of older persons (Renne, 1970). People suffering from physical disabilities, chronic conditions, or physical symptoms are more likely to be dissatisfied with their marriages. Educational level has little effect on marital satisfaction of older whites; however, older blacks with an eighth grade education or less are not as likely to be dissatisfied as those with a higher level of education (Renne, 1970). Affluence may be the critical factor in the marital satisfaction of older white wives.

Marital satisfaction is also positively associated with a general feeling of well-being, a positive view of one's health, and satisfaction with one's job, and negatively associated with heavy drinking, feelings of isolation and depression, and an absence of intimate associates (Renne, 1970). Lynn Caine, author of *Widow*, found a surprising number of married women attending her discussions on the topic, "Women Alone—How to Make Life Meaningful." These women considered themselves as alone as the widowed, divorced, or single women in the group. "They are lonely women, without a secure identity of their own, women who—deprived of love and recognition—are dying spiritually" (Caine, 1978, p. 51).

Another important factor influencing the marital satisfaction of the older woman is the effect of the husband's retirement on the couple's relationship. The wives who are sad about the retirement tend to be older, in poorer physical health, less active, more unhappy in their marriages and in general, and have husbands in manual occupations (Heyman and Jeffers, 1968). Wives of men who retired for health reasons or who have been retired over ten years are more often sorry than glad about the retirement.

Wives who feel pessimistic about their husbands' retirement are concerned that their husbands have lost their major interest in life. The husbands have too much time on their hands and intrude into the domestic domain of the wife. Women who see no adjustment problems in their husbands' retirement view retirement as a time for a new and exciting life together (Fengler, 1975). Increased companionship and shared activities and interests, such as hobbies, travel, and visiting children and grandchildren, give them more time together. These women see their husbands as having hobbies that keep them busy and active.

A woman now in her 60s has a long-established self-image. The basic image is usually that of wife, homemaker, and retired mother. "Her overt role has consisted in establishing the tone of the home, doing or managing the housework, planning and purchasing, giving her husband sympathy and support in his work, and in earlier years rearing children" (Cavan, 1968, pp. 464–465). She often has friends, activities, and interests that do not include her husband.

In order to maintain his image as competent, decisive, and productive, the retired husband may assume new decision-making roles in the home or may become a self-appointed authority in areas heretofore the woman's major areas of expertise. The wife's raison d'être is threatened, and conflict is inevitable.

One means of adaptation for the retired male is the creation of a new role to replace the occupational one (Lipman, 1961). In households where husbands participated but did not take over household tasks, the couple's morale was considerably higher than in households where the husband did not participate (Kerckhoff, 1966). This new role included many household chores that could be performed jointly, especially chores requiring little specialized skill and knowledge. As the husband became involved in household activities, the wife would no longer view her primary role as one of housekeeper and homemaker. The couple moved toward a common area of activities, with an emphasis on sharing and cooperation. Love, understanding, companionship, and compatibility became the most important things a couple could give each other (Cavan, 1968). These adjustments worked out very well, particularly if the couple's desire for full-time work diminished with increasing age. In the future, with increasing emphasis on role equality and companionship in marriage, greater numbers of wives may look more favorably on their husbands' retirement (Fengler, 1975).

DISPLACED HOMEMAKERS

Most women who are now in their fifties and sixties bought the social contract of man the breadwinner and woman the homemaker. They assumed that their retirement benefits, health insurance, and economic security flowed from their marriage (Sommers and Shields, 1978, p. 91).

Homemaking is still the full-time occupation of a majority of married women. Displaced homemakers are usually middle-aged women who have worked in the home for a substantial number of years providing unpaid household service for family members. They have not been employed outside the home on a regular basis. They have been displaced from their homemaking role through separation, divorce, or widowhood.

For a number of reasons, displaced homemakers are often left without any source of financial security. They are ineligible for social security benefits because they are too young. They are not eligible for federal welfare assistance if they are not physically disabled of if their children are over 18. They do not qualify for unemployment insurance because they have been engaged in unpaid labor in the home. Often they have lost their rights as beneficiaries under employers' pension and health plans even though contributing years to maintaining the family well-being (Task Force on Older Women, 1975). They are often subject to discrimination in employment because of age, sex, and lack of any recent paid work experience.

The actual number of women who qualify as displaced homemakers is not known. Tish Sommers, the coordinator of the National Organization for Women's Task Force on Older Women estimates that as of 1975 there were between two million and three million displaced homemakers (Katz, 1975). Fifteen million women not in the labor market who currently have children will be without benefits when their children reach age 18 (Sommers and Shields, 1978). Thus, the problem is likely to increase. Major factors contributing to the potential increase are changes in the family structure, increased life expectancy of women, and changes in society as a whole.

Traditional aids that society has provided in the past are decreasing (Katz, 1975). Alimony payments are not as large as often imagined; in addition, the trend is toward no-fault divorce and spouse support payments for a limited period, if at all. A report by the National Commission on the Observance of International Women's Year stated that only 14 percent of divorced women are awarded alimony. "Of these, only 45 percent get their payment with any degree of regularity" (Sommers and Shields, 1978, p. 91). With increasing inflation, a husband's life insurance and other assets may not provide a widow with the financial security he had expected.

Displaced homemakers need jobs, yet most cannot compete in today's job market. They have no recent record of employment and often are victims of age discrimination. Their skills may be obsolete or underdeveloped. Thus, job training and placement are essential services for the displaced homemaker. Other services that are important are: counseling, health screening, money-management courses, and resource referral.

Two displaced homemaker centers—one in Baltimore, Maryland, and the other in Oakland, California—now provide services focused on the needs of former homemakers. In the spring of 1975, a displaced home-makers's bill was introduced in the U.S. House of Representatives but was not enacted. In 1978 Congress added displaced homemakers as a category of the hard-to-employ under Titles II, III, and VII of the newly authorized Comprehensive Employment and Training Act. Whether this new form of legislation will provide a viable nationwide program for former homemakers remains to be seen (Sommers and Sheilds, 1978).

DIVORCE

An increasing number of couples are divorcing after 20 or more years of marriage. In 1964 164,000 divorces were granted to people 45 years and older. "By 1974, the annual number had nearly doubled to 315,000" (Rooney, 1978, p. 6). When asked about the cause of the divorce, most couples said that the problems were always there in the background. When the children had grown and left home, trouble erupted, and divorce followed.

The impact of divorce on the lives of older women has not been studied in depth. Displaced Homemaker Centers in Maryland and California offer counseling and job-seeking skills to older homemakers who have been displaced from their role by divorce or widowhood. (The legal aspects of divorce are discussed together with those of widowhood in the next section, on widowhood.)

WIDOWHOOD

"American society has given scant attention to the problems of widowhood. Beyond a minimal awareness that the widowhood may have financial problems, for which social security assistance may be available, there has been little interest in what it means to be widowed" (Abrahams, 1972, p. 54). The average age at which widowhood occurs in America is 56 years (Bengtson, Kasschau, and Ragan, 1977). Frequently, widows today are faced with financial problems, the challenge of finding a fulfilling job (often after being a housewife for years), and the need to find new supportive personal relationships.

Widows aged 65 and over constitute 31 percent of all people aged 65 years and over and 53 percent of all elderly women (U.S. DHEW, 1976). There are three principal reasons for the existence of such a large number of elderly widows. One is the high mortality rate for males of all ages. Another is the disparity in ages between husbands and wives. On the average, 81 percent of husbands aged 65 and older were 4 years older than their wives (U.S. DHEW, 1976). A third reason for the large numbers of elderly widows is the limited opportunity to remarry because of the relatively small number of eligible males over age 65. In addition, these men often marry women from younger age groups, while widows are not expected to marry men younger than themselves.

Widowhood is a personal crisis of major import. The widow must deal with her immediate grief, financial and legal aspects of the situation, changes in her social relationships, and other individual problems. The adjustment to the enduring role change from being part of a pair to being alone is a significant dimension of widowhood.

Death and Dying

Many factors in our culture conspire to remove death from our minds and feelings. The emphasis is on the preservation of youth and the denial of dying. In our life styles we have less contact with nature, with the daily struggle for life by the animals in the forest and field, and with the slaughtering of animals (Krupp and Kligfeld, 1962). For example, few middle-aged and younger women today have had the experience of killing a chicken for dinner, while this was a common task for the farm wife of earlier times.

The development of antibiotics and new advances in surgery have increased the length of life; thus, many deaths of middle-aged as well as younger people have been prevented or postponed. This decreases the chance of any given individual having direct experience with death until relatively late in life (Stub, 1966). Hospital care for the terminally ill and the proliferation of nursing homes have encouraged the removal of many seriously sick and disabled older people from family, friends, and neighborhood circles; consequently, contact with the dying becomes less frequent. "When the dying are segregated among specialists for whom contact with death has become routine and even somewhat impersonal, neither their presence while alive nor as corpses interferes greatly with the mainstream of life" (Blauner, 1968, p. 535).

Older people are less fearful of contemplating death than is commonly believed (Smith, 1973). However, few openly admit to a fear of death. Looking forward to death or evading thinking about the experience are common attitudes. Several factors appear to be significantly related to a person's attitude toward death (Swenson, 1961). Religion seems to play a very important role in an aging person's attitude toward death. Older people who engage in little religious activity tend to have more fearful attitudes toward death, while older people with more fundamental religious convictions are more likely to look forward to death. Individuals living alone more often fear death than those living in homes for the aged or with relatives. For older women one study reported a negative relationship between a sense of purpose in life and fear of death (Durlak, 1973).

Less educated people tend to have evasive attitudes toward death, while those who have finished college tend to express a more direct attitude toward death, either fearing it or looking forward to it (Swenson, 1961). Widowhood and good health are other characteristics that may be related to an evasive attitude about death.

It is often the fear of dying alone or of being forgotten, rather than the fear of death itself, that torments the older person who is dying (Smith, 1973). The dying may experience loneliness and a feeling of abandonment because others avoid thinking about death and are unwilling to tell the patient about the gravity of the illness. Most of the evidence indicates that most dying people are aware of their condition and want to talk about their anxieties, fears, and concerns (Brody, 1974).

There is individuality in the way a person copes with and adapts to the possibility of death (Brody, 1974). The dying person often experiences a complex range of emotions and reactions—among them intense fear, anxiety, anger, depression, defeat, helplessness, and hopelessness. However, some very old people approach the end of their lives with relative equanimity. Additional research evidence suggests that women are more distressed by the impact of their illness and death on others, while men are more disturbed by pain, dependency, and loss of occupational role (Kastenbaum, 1974).

The dying process may be, but is not always, a time of crisis. A chaotic state during terminal illness may be caused by mismanaged treatment of the patient (Kastenbaum, 1975). Lieberman (1968) suggests that the psychological changes preceding death may cause disruption in a person's mental process, shown by a decreased ability to cope with the demands of the environment. This may be particularly caused by a lowered ability to organize and integrate stimuli. Thus, the person may experience upheaval because of disrupted mental processes rather than fear of death. "Individuals approaching death pull away from those around them, not because of a narcissistic preoccupation with themselves, but because they are preoccupied with an attempt to hold themselves together—to reduce the experience to chaos" (Lieberman, 1968, p. 518).

In the process of controlling death, our society has made it difficult for people to die with dignity. People no longer die at home in familiar and meaningful surroundings, with family and friends. The hospital atmosphere serves to remove the dying person from life even before death occurs. Modern medical advances have made it possible for body functions to be performed artificially by machines. Yet, in the case of incurable illness, most older people do not want their lives prolonged.

Many older people are asking not just for days of existence but for the ability to live and die in such a way that their humanity and sense of communion with others be maintained. They ask to die as they have lived—with a sense of oneness with the world (Smith, 1973, p. 144).

Bereavement   "The funeral 'parlor,' the banks of flowers heaped around the coffin, the make-up used on the deceased, the music, and even the words spoken by many ministers tend to deny death and the possibility that it is happening to ourselves and our loved ones. Friends look at the corpse and describe it as 'so lifelike' " (Krupp and Kligfeld, 1962, p. 227). In our culture, the mourning period has few rituals outside of the funeral. Participation in funerals is usually limited to family members and friends rather than open to the larger community, as in more primitive societies (Blauner, 1968). Adaptation to bereavement has become a private responsibility. Thus, the widow must adjust to changes in her role and status largely through her own efforts. This individualization and deritualization of bereavement is likely to result in adjustment problems.

The bereavement period can be reviewed as a series of stages covering the time period from the intial shock through the rebuilding of a new life (Silverman, 1972). In the initial stage the widow is numb. She often appears calm and able to cope with the various responsibilities connected with the funeral and other matters. She still acts as if she were her husband's wife, and does not think of herself as a widow. This period may last as long as one month, but a much shorter time is usual.

As the numbness fades, the widow begins to feel the pain created by the awareness that the husband is gone permanently. She frequently "sees" and talks with her dead husband. She may have a variety of feelings: anger, bitterness, guilt, abandonment, and self-hatred. A feeling of falling apart or losing emotional control is common. Friends often stay away because they don't know what to do. The widow, who is feeling unloved and unlovable, may not respond well to visitors. Yet those friends who persist fill a major need for her during this period of mourning. One year is the average extent of acute bereavement.

Widows who have recently suffered bereavement must be allowed to express grief over the loss of their husbands. They need to be encouraged to cry, talk about their late husbands, and tell how badly they feel. This "grief work" described by Lindemann (1944) appears to be the most important need of recent widows.

The widow does not recover from her grief; rather she must make an accommodation or adjustment. Having time to prepare for the loss of a spouse may not make the adjustment to widowhood easier. "Any verbal discussion of what widowhood involves rarely occurs even when the spouse is seriously ill and death is anticipated" (Silverman, 1972, p. 95). Older widows who experienced an extended period of grief in anticipation of a spouse's death adjusted no better to the loss than those who experienced the sudden loss of a spouse (Gerber, 1975). "A woman's sense of self is changed and the very nature of her outer world is different" (Silverman, 1972). As the widow begins to have longer periods of feeling better, she may set new goals and develop renewed interests in men and sex.

Lopata (1975a) found evidence of a different form of bereavement period in the lives of the Chicago widows she studied. For them the process of bereavement often did not evolve in orderly stages from shock to final acceptance and the rebuilding of a new life. The bereavement involved many unpleasant events of different types coming from several directions, thus provoking feelings of frustration, helplessness, and a sense of being pulled apart. Sometimes loss of income meant dependence on relatives or welfare and perhaps moving from the family home. Other family problems did not cease because of the death of the husband. The new widow often felt incapable of coping with serious problems and making decisions on her own.

Another dimension of the early bereavement period noted by Lopata (1975a) is extreme satisfaction with the dead husband and with the marriage. The husband becomes an unusually fine man who treated his wife with respect, was a good companion, and had no irritating habits. In metropolitan areas, the funeral procedures appeared to encourage this satisfaction.

Legal Aspects of Widowhood

Inheritance and property laws may be detrimental to older women. Inheritance and property laws fall within the purview of state, rather than federal, authority. Despite disparities among states, some commonalities exist. Widows' inheritance and property rights depend primarily on whether legal residence is established in a community property state or a common-law state.

A common misconception revolves around the notion that all property is jointly owned by a married couple, and that a spouse automatically acquires half the property on divorce or all the property on widowhood. This is not the case.

Community property states classify property in two ways. *Community* property is any property or possession acquired by the couple during their marriage. *Separate* property refers to any property or possessions owned by either partner before marriage. It can also refer to property one spouse receives during marriage by gift or inheritance. Such property must remain separate if it is to be considered the property of one individual. If a woman puts her inheritance money or trust funds into a joint account in both her and her husband's name, the separate property is said to be *commingled*, and it becomes community property. The law treats any property for which ownership is cloudy and not easily ascertained as community property.

When divorce occurs, each spouse retains his or her own separate property and the community property is shared equally. When either spouse dies, the survivor automatically owns one-half of the property. The deceased cannot will away more than his or her own half. Taxes cannot be levied on more than one-half of the estate, should a widow inherit her husband's estate, since she legally owns the other half (Alexander, 1975). There are currently eight community property states: Arizona, California, Idaho, Louisiana, Nevada, New Mexico, Texas, and Washington.

Forty-two states and the District of Columbia are common-law states. A wife in a common-law state does not automatically own half of all earnings and property accumulated during the marriage. The inequity of this law arises out of the woman's role as wife, mother, and homemaker. Filling those roles may, in fact, allow the husband to earn the income to acquire property, but if a woman cannot prove that she has contributed half of the dollars necessary to purchase property, she is not considered a coowner. Even in cases where a house is held in joint names, there is no guarantee that she will not have to pay an inheritance tax on it. She has "inherited" it from her husband because he paid for it.

It is wise practice for spouses to execute wills since in a common-law state there is no guarantee that the surviving spouse will automatically inherit an estate. The laws concerning *intestacy* (dying without a will) vary from state to state.

Estate taxes are generally paid to the federal government and to the state in which legal residence has been established. Federal taxes are based on the size of the net estate. The value of the gross is determined, and the widow (or whoever inherits the estate) is allowed to deduct certain items that are not included in the taxable estate. These deductions include burial expenses, claims against the estate by creditors, and the cost of administering the estate. Additionally, some states permit a widow to draw a living allowance while the estate is probated. (Some jurisdictions refer to the net estate as the adjusted gross estate.)

The Tax Reform Act of 1976 allows either a $250,000 marital deduction or a marital deduction of half the value of the adjusted gross estate, whichever is greater, and provides a tax credit against estate tax liabilities. This tax credit was $30,000 in 1977 and will escalate to $47,000 in 1981 (Lemov, 1977). This act corrects inequities that had often forced widows to sell their homes in order to pay the federal estate taxes.

Income adequacy is an essential factor to be considered in the adjustment to widowhood (Atchley, 1975). The husband's death often removes the wife's main source of income. Inadequate income can create social isolation because of the inability to own a car and to pay membership and other fees of social organizations. The resulting social isolation may produce anxiety, which in turn may precipitate emotional crises.

The situation of many elderly widows is particularly grim. As of March 1975 there were 6.5 million widows 65 years and over who were noninstitutionalized; of these, 62 percent were living alone (U.S. DHEW, 1976). Elderly widows generally have a low financial status and a higher rate of isolation than other segments of the over-65 population. "The median 1974 income of husband-wife families with the elderly head was $7,200, over 2½ times as large as the $2,700 reported for elderly women who do not have husbands and must rely primarily on their own income" (DHEW, 1976, p.

3). As of 1970 most elderly females living alone did not have regular use of an automobile; thus, they depended on public transportation for social contacts outside of their neighborhoods and for reaching a variety of services they often needed.

Role Adjustment to Widowhood

> The widows are talented, proud women. Most have spent their lives as housewives, and have few marketable job skills to start a new life. Even for those who do, jobs are hard to find. Their married friends exclude them from social gatherings. The widows cluster together; they have no alternative. Each has her own story of loneliness to tell, her own bitterness to bear. The small town both comforts and traps them (Peterson, 1979, p. 13).

Modern society provides few social roles for a widow who, therefore, has to search for a new definition of herself as a single person and create a social role for herself other than that of a wife. It is difficult to move out of the widowhood phase; American society has socialized present-day older women to be wives and mothers and has not encouraged alternative identities (Lopata, 1975c).

In some cultures the husband's brother is required to marry the widow. No such replacement provisions are available in the American culture. There is no social group which automatically takes over the roles carried out by the husband in the past (Lopata, 1975c).

Widowhood causes a major transformation in the social role of the older woman who is a housewife (Lopata, 1966). The removal of the role of wife is likely to be permanent, and mothering for the older widow is of little or no significance at this stage of life. The roles of worker and association member are not central parts of the housewife's life but may be significant for widows with careers or secure jobs.

Social interactions in the role of mother are limited. Almost one-fourth of Lopata's Chicago area respondents had no living children. "Barriers such as health deficiencies, economic limitations, and long distances diminish the widow's contact with children" (Lopata, 1970, p. 51). Most widows did not live with married children. The widows who supported themselves in their own homes reported greater peace, quiet, and independence.

Roles within kin groups were limited. Many of the women studied had no siblings. Over half of the women were not born in the Chicago area, so their brothers and sisters were scattered over the United States. The role of grandmother depends on the availability of direct contact with grandchildren without parental interference, in Lopata's view (1970).

Most of the older widows were not deeply involved in the roles of neighbor, worker, or member of voluntary associations. "The half who did have frequent interactions with people living nearby were restricted to seasonal, sporadic, and casual contact outside of the home" (Lopata, 1970, p. 55). Although theoretically many social roles are open to the American widow, Lopata (1970) found that factors related to race, health, finances, motivation, and ability serve to restrict the lives of widows.

Social Interactions

Arling (1976) surveyed 409 widows aged 65 and older who lived in the Piedmont area of South Carolina, to determine what factors were associated with a widow's ability to resist isolation in old age.

> Ill health and poverty, coupled with widowhood and the normal social losses of old age, confront the elderly widow with the prospect of becoming socially isolated. Her ability to resist this trend may be heightened by education, residence in a small town or rural area, or most importantly the presence of friends and neighbors with whom she can relate (Arling, 1976, p. 84).

Interestingly, in this analysis, family ties were not associated with daily activities, while friendship and neighboring were strongly related. "Even with economic deprivation, physical incapacity, and education held constant, those elderly widows who knew more of their neighbors and had greater contact with friends and neighbors also participated in more activities" (Arling, 1976, p. 84). Arling concludes that friends and neighbors are a better resource than family for avoiding isolation in old age.

Changes in social relationships also depend on the type of social relationship a widow has (Heyman and Gianturco, 1973). Relationships that do not involve the presence of a spouse, such as garden and bridge clubs, may continue with little or no change or interruption. Social networks involving relatives, neighbors, and friends from church groups remain intact.

Being widowed at an older age means that a settled social role with few job and family responsibilities has already been established. Also, there will be a larger number of widows within one's peer group. Therefore, the widow aged 70 and over is less likely to feel she belongs nowhere than the younger widow and less likely to decrease her social interactions

(Blau, 1956). Widows living in small towns retained nearly the same level of contact with family and friends and participation in activities (Pihlblad and Adams, 1972), while widows in Chicago became more isolated (Lopata, 1970). In sum, factors related to little or no change in the social interactions of widows are: relationships not involving a spouse, being widowed at an older age, a peer group of significant size, an established social role with few responsibilities, residence in a small town, and the presence of friends and neighbors.

Sex differences affect the social interactions of the widowed (Berardo, 1970). Particular dimensions of the traditional role of older women encourage continued social interactions: (1) the responsibility of maintaining kinship interactions; (2) the role of grandmother, which has a more meaningful range of activities than that of grandfather; and (3) preference for recreational activities that can be easily engaged in at older ages. In addition, the widow is more likely than the widower to be invited to live with one of her children.

The major factor in the amount of disruption in social interactions that a widow experiences is, in Lopata's (1970) view, the degree to which her social roles were dependent on her husband. This dependence was influenced by the characteristics of the couple's background and life. The more multidimensional the involvement of her husband in a women's life, the more disorganized became her other social relations with her husband's death. His death may remove a sexual partner, a partner in couple-oriented leisure activities, a contributor to the management of the home, a link to the outside world through community and business contacts that he maintained, and any other interactions in which her involvement depended on his.

The segment of the social structure and culture that widows are part of also influences their social relations. In researching forms of loneliness in her Chicago widows, Lopata (1969) concluded that the ability to plan a systematic program of activity and social contact "is very much a middle- and upper-class phenomenon, typical of women who have had a relatively extensive educational background and prior involvement in secondary groups" (p. 258). The ability to form new relations was also found mainly in the middle and upper classes.

Using the Chicago widows, Lopata (1973) studied the self-identity changes of married women who became widowed. As part of the study, she measured social isolation. The isolation of the women who scored high on the social isolation scale was not caused by the spouse's death but had been part of their life styles. Ninety-seven percent of the highly isolated women reported their social life to be the same as before the death of their husbands. These isolated widows had a minimum of education (less than 8 years). Educational achievement was correlated with ability to become socially active whether or not the husband was alive.

Blau's study (1961) also found that social class differences were evident in the social participation of widows. She suggested two reasons for these differences:

1. The middle-class widow has a reservoir of social opportunities created by a pattern of shared social activities with other women that supplemented her activities with her husband.
2. Widowhood for working-class women more often imposes severe economic deprivations that greatly limit social activities.

Few social activities, limited income, working-class membership, minimal education, residence in a metropolitan area, and little contact with friends and neighbors all are factors that may limit the social interactions of widows. Which, if any, of these factors is more significant than others has not been determined by extensive research.

Problems and Resources

All widows do not suffer from the same problems. Morgan (1976) suggests looking at the problems of widowhood rather than viewing widowhood as a problem. The sources of difficulty could be pinpointed and intervention strategies could be directed toward changing these situational difficulties.

The death of a spouse always disrupts the life style of the survivor, even if it has been expected for a long time. The extent of the disruption can be viewed in terms of: (1) the amount of dependence on the social, financial, and emotional support provided by the deceased; (2) the ways in which the married couple were involved with family, friends, and the community; (3) the resources and life style of the survivors; and (4) the actions taken by the surviving spouse (Lopata, 1975c).

The widow may have many needs. Financial and medical needs, lack of daily social interaction, and interrupted plans for the future may add to the stress of the bereavement period (Gerber, 1975). The short-range needs of the widow fall into five areas: expression of grief, companionship, solution of immediate problems, building of competence and self-confidence, and help in regaining connections with friends and activities (Lopata, 1975a).

The widow must also attempt to resolve the long-range issue of building a meaningful life as a single older woman. The enormity of being alone usually impacts upon the widow after the funeral. The distractions provided by planning for and going through the funeral and the myriad of friends and relatives who must be fed and housed are no longer available to shield her from the realization that her husband has exited from her life.

The process of dealing with the pain of sudden singleness is not easily dealt with. The widow rides an emotional roller coaster. Anger, and guilt, are familiar themes. The widow rages against the doctor who was unable to save her husband, against coworkers who were not astute enough to recognize symptoms and so failed to intervene, against a God that took a good man while others less worthy were allowed to live, and even against the dead husband who deserted her and shattered her world. The widow also feels guilty that she did not do more for her husband while he was alive. She convinces herself that had she been a better wife he would be alive today.

The widow also tends to think she is going crazy. Most widows retain an old piece of their husband's clothing and wear it because it makes them feel less alone. They may continue a behavior pattern that included the husband while he was alive, such as mixing his predinner cocktail and leaving it next to his easy chair even though he is no longer alive. Some widows think they see their husband at a distance or in a crowd while others believe that the deceased talks to them.

At the same time that the widow is experiencing profound emotional turmoil, friends and relatives usually withdraw, leaving the widow with minimal emotional support. The time when she needs friends most is generally the time when they are least accessible. This is due in part to the widow's reluctance to accept invitations. Eventually the invitations are no longer extended.

Friends also withdraw because the widow is perceived as a threat. A single woman does not fit into a couples-oriented social group. She serves as a reminder that no one is protected from the possibility of losing a husband.

Support of an emotional, physical, or financial nature from children living in close proximity decreases the chance of depression as a result of widowhood (Clayton et al., 1972). Various mutual help programs involving widows are now in action in various parts of the United States. These may involve actual contact by widowed volunteers with the newly widowed or may be a telephone service to aid widows in solving problems concerning finances, jobs, loneliness, loving arrangements, health, and so forth (Abrahams, 1972; Silverman, 1972).

Lopata (1979) sees American widows 60 years and older as having problems that are unique in many ways. She delineates these problems as follows (p. 383):

1. Inability to earn an income and high probability of poverty, as well as inadequate development and information about part-time jobs.
2. Agism, or stereotyping people by age.
3. Inadequate background due to the traditional limitations imposed on women.
4. Inadequate facilities in many communities for social contact with peers.
5. Fear of rejection, which decreases the probability of using existing resources.
6. Sexual imbalance making male companionship very rare; the older the woman, the fewer men are available for egalitarian interaction. Assumption of absence of sexual and other intimacy desires.
7. Inadequate, often dangerous, housing—a barrier to social contact.
8. Lack of contacts to prevent or handle emergencies, such as daily calls or a "hot line."
9. If relatively house-bound, lack of social contact; lack of medical and dental care; and lack of adequate nutrition.

Traditional socialization and limited education have failed to equip many of these women for living competently in the world today. Traditional supports in the form of a constantly present family and an unchanging neighborhood are rapidly disappearing.

Our society offers a vast network of resources such as: social service and health care agencies, voluntary associations, jobs, friendships outside the family, and self-help groups. Yet these older urban widows generally are not able to use such resources to build their own new support systems. They are hampered by the lack of self-confidence or by a negative view of any aggressive attempts to change their life styles. Any feelings of self-sufficiency and positive self-regard are more likely to come from the woman herself rather than from contacts with confidants, community activities, or agencies.

Opportunities for flexible and complex social involvement by women

have expanded dramatically during the past 60 years, so that newer generations of women may face fewer of the problems and restrictions of today's
older urban widow. More will have the ability to use various resources to
build their own new support systems when widowed.

Although few widows at present lead multidimensional lives, change
may be in the offing:

> What may be happening, is that women freed from the controls of the family
> institutions through widowhood may be purposely disrupting the vestiges of
> their prior role clusters after the "grief work" is done and entering roles and
> lifestyles that they never would have considered in girlhood and wifehood,
> becoming independent functioning units rather than being dependent upon
> passive acceptance of membership in units dominated by others (Lopata,
> 1975c, p. 233).

Remarriage

Remarriage as an option for older women who want to live in a family
situation has become an important issue. Changes in life expectancy have
increased the number of older women. Divorce among older women is
increasing. Many of the children of older women, themselves in the
postparental stage and facing retirement, may be unable or unwilling to
provide a home for an aging parent. Ethnic groups whose traditions dictate
that widowed parents live with their children are decreasing in number.

Social norms do not support the remarriage of older widowed people.
Children are especially likely to discourage a parent's remarriage. In some
cases children fear their share of an inheritance will be reduced. Also, most
children have thought of their parents only in the roles of mother and
father, not husband and wife. "The sudden role reversal in which they are
asked to accept a new member in the family is beyond their comprehension
and they begin to consider their parent as childish, perverse, and certainly
not qualified to select a marriage partner" (McKain, 1972, p. 62).

The factors that relate to a successful marriage after retirement age
are summarized by McKain (1969) under six headings:

1. Bride and groom know each other well.
2. The marriage is approved by the children and friends of the
   couple.
3. Both people easily adjust to the withdrawal from some roles that
   takes place at this point in life.

4. Both the bride and groom own a home, so that they come to the marriage on equal terms.
5. Both the bride and groom have sufficient income.
6. Both the husband and wife are reasonably well-adjusted individuals.

Even if older women were encouraged to marry, many would not find a mate. They need to find other types of family situations. Sharing of a home by two or more women provides companionship of peers and fulfills dependency needs in times of financial or physical stress. Adult children of a close friend or foster grandchildren also can provide a personal family relationship.

THE GRANDMOTHER ROLE

The changes that have taken place in the timing of events in the family life cycle as a result of earlier marriages and earlier and more closely spaced childbearing has made grandparenting a middle-age, rather than an old-age, phenomenon (Wood and Robertson, 1976). Women may now become greatgrandmothers in their old age. Two new styles of grandparenting are more frequently being enacted by present-day grandmothers. One is characterized as a fun-seeking relationship, while the other is labeled a "distant" relationship (Neugarten and Weinstein, 1968).

In the fun-seeking relationship, the grandparent joins the child in specific activities for the particular purpose of having fun. Grandchildren are perceived as a source of leisure activity or as a source of self-indulgence. The emphasis is on a mutually satisfying relationship.

The other style is that of a grandparent who has infrequent contact with the grandchildren, appearing only on holidays and other special occasions. "This grandparent is benevolent in stance but essentially distant and remote from the child's life, a somewhat intermittent St. Nicholas" (Neugarten and Weinstein, 1968, p. 284).

Women under age 65 more often adopt the fun-seeking style of grandparenting, while those over 65 more frequently have a distant relationship with their grandchildren. The relationship between age differences and grandparenting style may reflect differences in values and expectations in persons who grow up and grow old at different times in history (Neugarten and Weinstein, 1968). Another explanation for the age differences may be that processes of aging and/or continuing socialization produce behavior changes over time in the grandparenting role. Only a study following grandparenting over both periods of time would provide information about whether grandparenting style is a cohort phenomenon or a style that changes with age.

"Women often describe a preparatory period in which they visualize themselves as grandmothers, often before their children are married" (Neugarten and Weinstein, 1968, p. 285). They may relive their own pregnancies and childbearing experiences in anticipation of the birth of a grandchild. However, the expectation of grandmothering as welcome and pleasurable is frequently accompanied by doubts of being "ready" and feelings of being forced into old age by the appearance of the grandchild.

Older women may see the grandparenting role as one socially acceptable avenue for involvement with their children's families. Grandmothers often take on major household responsibilities when the mother is giving birth or working or in times of illness and crisis. A majority of grandmothers find grandparenting comfortable and pleasant, but a sizable minority feel disappointment, discomfort, or lack of positive rewards from the role (Neugarten and Weinstein, 1968).

Women more often than men find the grandparenting role a way of feeling young again (Neugarten and Weinstein, 1968). The Foster Grandparent Program (described in Chapter 5) has been a very successful volunteer activity. However research appears to indicate that the role has only limited significance to many older people. Grandparents usually live on the fringe of the family group and assume a vital function only in the case of the disruption of the family functioning. "Overall, grandparents do not seem to expect tangible commitments from their grandchildren; they appear to be content if their grandchildren give them a modicum of interest and concern, however ritualistic or superficial this may be" (Wood and Robertson, 1976, p. 302).

PARENT-CHILD RELATIONSHIPS

Older women are expected to want to have continuous meaningful contact with their children and other relatives but not to want to live with them. This type of relationship is characterized as "intimacy at a distance" (Streib, 1972). A number of research studies have found that most older people have close relatives within easy visiting distance and contacts are frequent (Lowenthal and Robinson, 1976).

Close relationships with children do not necessarily boost the morale of aging parents (Blau, 1973; Kerckhoff, 1966). The norm that precludes older people making demands on the young may prevent them from expressing close interpersonal needs to their adult children. Sterility, formality, and ritualism seem to characterize the relationships of many adult children and their parents (Lowenthal and Robinson, 1976). It may be that adult children see involvement with parents as preventing them from living their own lives. The parents reinforce this idea by saying that their children have to live their own lives. The ill health of older people may increase the amount of interaction, but the sickness may eventually alienate family members who are fearful of being burdened with the care. Unwell women and men often are dissatisfied with their relationships with their children and lack close relationships with their grandchildren (Maas and Kuypers, 1974).

In the near future women in their 60s will be faced with caring for infirm parents, especially mothers in their 80s and 90s, if they are not already faced with this situation. The demands of their parents, on the one hand, and the demands of their grandchildren, on the other, may weaken a woman's relationships with both (Lowenthal and Robinson, 1976). The aging parent needs support in experiences such as the loss of her spouse or increasing disability. Effective means of coping with physical problems must be planned.

When the parents have been unable to meet the child's needs for affection and dependency, the care of the parent by the grown child may be responsibly performed but resented. In families where the parents have been relatively stable emotionally and able to respond adequately to the needs of a growing child, the child's positive feelings toward the parents continue into old age, despite the physical and personality changes the years might bring (Simos, 1970).

SUMMARY

An older woman today can expect to live several decades beyond the time when her youngest child leaves home. Changes in the family relationships of older women are caused by factors such as children leaving home, the husband's retirement, separation and divorce, and aging parents.

Most women experience change in their family roles earlier than men because of these women's involvement in homemaking and child-rearing as primary tasks. The period after the children leave home may be a time when women set new goals for their lives, find new ways to continue the nurturing role, or feel a sense of emptiness not easily filled. Reactions depend on the individual woman's characteristics and her life situation. Many women do not feel that children leaving home creates a crisis period.

The marital satisfaction in older women's lives is influenced by a number of factors. Children leaving home may give the parents a sense of freedom from responsibility, and interest in the marriage relationship may increase. The effect of the husband's retirement on the couple's relationship is another important influence. Health, job satisfaction, and financial conditions also have impacts on marital satisfaction.

Changes in the marital and homemaking roles because of widowhood, separation, and divorce have created the "displaced homemaker." Displaced homemakers are usually middle-aged women who have not been employed on a regular basis outside the home; they have provided unpaid household services to family members for a substantial number of years. They often need job training and placement in order to be able to create their own financial security.

Widowhood and divorce affect increasing numbers of older women. In the United States in 1976 more than half of women age 65 and over are widows. The divorce rate among couples who have been married 20 years or longer is on the increase. Between 1964 and 1974 the annual number of divorces granted to people 45 years and older has almost doubled.

Widowhood and divorce are personal crises of major import. Women experiencing such crises must adjust to the change in roles from wives to single women. They may find themselves with a more independent life style than any they would have considered previously. Many older women do not have the option of remarriage because of the shorter life expectancy of men and older men's tendency to marry younger women. Women who want to live in family situations need to consider other possibilities, such as sharing a home with other women.

Women now become grandmothers during middle age rather than at old age because of marriage at earlier ages and more closely spaced childbearing. The grandmother role can be a socially acceptable way for an older woman to become involved with her children and can be a way for her to feel young again. However being a grandmother appears to have only limited importance in the lives of older women.

A woman's family relationships may grow more complex as she ages. Maintaining meaningful contact with her children may be hindered by the children's view of such involvement as preventing them from living their own lives. Needs and desires of the woman's parents and parents-in-law also may have a strong impact on the nature of her family relationships. In the future, more women reaching their 60s will face caring for infirm parents, in particular mothers who are over age 80. If positive feelings between children and parents are developed during childhood, these feelings are likely to continue into the parents' old age despite the physical and personality changes that the years may bring.

■7
Employment and Retirement

WORK ASPIRATION AND CHOICE

Defining the meaning of work for women has been a difficult task; the American social system traditionally has not prepared many women adequately for involvement in the paid labor force. The literature that analyzes and describes American occupational involvement is based on studies of men at work. As a result, the different work patterns of women are poorly understood.

Value systems change slowly; American women are still not expected to consider work outside the home as an equal alternative to their "natural" roles of wife and mother, nor as parallel to these roles. Work is viewed as a secondary role for women, regardless of age or familial status. Work is accepted as a primary role only in the lives of older unmarried women. Despite a cultural value system that restricts women's orientation toward work and their employment in occupations, women are joining the labor force in unprecedented numbers.

In this chapter we will examine the meaning of work for women and explore some of the factors that maintain women in traditional work settings. Continuing education, an action strategy for breaking out of traditional patterns, is discussed. Finally, the psychological and economic adjustments required by women at the time of their retirement will be presented.

Trends in Labor Force Participation

Changes in labor force participation have been far more dramatic for women than for men and have had impact across all age groups. A recent study finds that "the interesting new trend is that middle-aged women, having outgrown their limitations of interest, are now returning to school and even preparing for professions in dramatic numbers" (Lopata and Steinhart, 1971, p. 30). This is especially interesting since middle-aged and older women belong to those cohort groups socialized to believe that they would become wives and mothers rather than working women.

The number of women workers doubled between 1950 and 1974. Forty-six percent of all women 16 years of age and over were in the labor force in 1974, and now women account for nearly 40 percent of all workers (U.S. Dept. of Labor, 1975). At the same time that female participation has increased, the labor force participation by men has declined.

In 1974 married women living with their spouses accounted for 22.4 percent of the total labor force, or nearly 58 percent of all women in the labor force. Divorce, separation, and widowhood also affect labor-force activity. Participation by these groups, as well as by never-married women, comprises 16 percent of the total labor force, or 42 percent of all women in the labor force. Projections of the size of the labor force by sex and age indicate that by 1990 there may be 43.7 million women in the labor force, a 22 percent increase over the 35.9 million women in the labor force in 1974 (U.S. Dept. of Commerce, 1976a).

Discrimination in Employment

Despite the increasing numbers of women in the labor force, employers still exhibit a great degree of resistance to hiring older women. Such women are perceived to be "menopausal," "hysterical," "unreliable," "untrainable," and so forth. The evidence indicates that older women are more reliable than younger women (Kreps and Clark, 1975). They have lower rates of absenteeism and are more willing to learn new tasks. Tradition and cultural bias, however, dominate the views of employers.

The incomes of women workers tend to be less than those of their male counterparts. Women workers aged 45 to 54 earn 54 percent of the amount earned by comparably aged men; in the 55 to 64 age bracket, women earn 61 percent as much as like-aged men.

Such wage discrepancies are due to several factors. First, women with no marketable skills, or outmoded skills, are only eligible for jobs requiring little experience or training, which are, of course, accompanied by low pay.

Forty-eight percent of women over 45 are employed in the areas of retail sales, unskilled or semiskilled factory work, private household work, and other service jobs. Another 28 percent of women over 45 are involved in clerical work.

Second, women have traditionally had less formal education than men. In 1950, when today's middle-aged woman would have matriculated into college, the cultural belief that she would be provided for by a husband often prevented her from completing an education and pursuing a career. Half as many women as men enrolled in college in 1950, and only 61 percent of those women completed four years. Older women entering the labor force today, therefore, are at a disadvantage in terms of where they start and in terms of future promotional opportunities. Women have attempted to overcome this handicap by enrolling in continuing education programs in increasing numbers, as discussed later in this chapter.

Third, most women have had extended nonwork periods when they raised children and managed households. Their limited numbers of years of employment act to depress the income ceiling they will achieve before retirement.

Finally, the lesser wages often reflect employer bias, and the belief that most middle-aged women are working because they want to fill their time. In fact, most older women work because they need the money. Single women have to support themselves; many also support dependents. Married women may be required to contribute to college tuition, care of aging or ill parents, mortgage payments, or may need to ensure an adequate retirement income.

Continuing Education

In general, continuing education is perceived to be the resumption of education by the mature woman, although apparently no one definition of what constitutes a mature woman is acceptable to all. While the Department of Labor defines the mature woman as one over 45 years old, reports on continuing education programs for the mature woman have not adhered to this view. It is more or less accepted that the mature woman and the older woman are one and the same, but the age at which one is considered mature or older varies anywhere from 25 years to over 35 years.

The probable cause behind the disparity in definitions is the lack of statistical data in education on women over the age of 35. Few studies on the mature woman in continuing education have made efforts to differentiate between the educational needs, interests, and goals of 30-, 40-, 50-, and 60-year-old women who are resuming their educational pursuits. In some studies, mature women are classified into two categories: those between the ages of 25 and 35 and those over 35.

Although it would be unrealistic to make a blanket statement about who the older, mature returnees are, the picture of these women as presented by various studies and reports on continuing education programs indicates that they have much in common. For the most part the continuing education programs still serve middle-aged, middle-income, and middle-class women, although an increasing number are older women from low-income and minority groups.

The motivating forces accounting for the sudden increase in the number of older women returning to school can be attributed to factors that are both within and beyond the capacity for women to change. Given the social and economic conditions of the changing times, women are finding themselves in a situation which they had not foreseen. Because 20 is the average age when women marry, by the time they reach midlife their children are in school or living on their own. Modern household conveniences leave the housewife with time on her hands; with less and less to do in the home, she is apt to be overcome with dissatisfaction and boredom.

For some older women, this period in their lives becomes a time to reassess their roles as wives, mothers, and women. Beginning to have self-doubts and wanting to once again be valued and important, these women often turn to the school for redirection. They expect that education will fill the void in their lives while bringing them personal enrichment and a more meaningful relationship with the surrounding world. This is also true for returning women who are divorced or having marital problems. For these women, pursuing their educational endeavors is either a financial or psychological necessity, or both.

The anticipation of a career change that brings a possible financial gain also draws the older woman back to school. The resumption of an education as preparation to reenter the work force entails the updating of rusty skills or the acquisition of new ones.

Whether the reasons for the return of the mature woman to the campus are academic interest or vocational pursuit, whether the reasons are social or cultural, the fact remains that the number of mature women attending colleges and universities is rising. Of the 1.3 million college students over the age of 34 in 1978, about two-thirds were women (Rich, 1979). These women have shown the desire and motivation to obtain further education.

Most attempts to assist the returning older woman have been through counseling services. These women are confronted with problems that are unique to their situation. In deciding to resume their education or strive for a career, these women must often face negative or mixed reactions from their families and the general public sentiment that a woman's place is in the home. While some families support the woman returnee, others create an atmosphere that promotes feelings of guilt and inadequacy in the returning woman. Guilt may also develop because the mother and housewife is spending more time away from home and comes to feel that she is failing her family.

The inner and outer conflicts that accompany many women who return to college in midlife probably account for one of the major findings of studies on continuing education; the older woman almost overwhelmingly has a very low self-concept and has little confidence in her ability to perform scholastically or to make the necessary adjustments to academic life. Even women who once graduated with honors at age 21 will at age 40 feel inadequate and tentative when first undertaking graduate work. Adjustments are further hampered by frequent encounters with age and sex discrimination or routines designed for younger students only that tend to isolate the older student from the rest of the academic community. Fortunately, many colleges now offer counseling services and group discussions for older students, allowing them the opportunity to interact, to realize that they are not alone, and helping them to a realistic appraisal of their competence.

Not only does the older returnee have to deal with her psychological needs, she must also cope with her many practical needs. She must attend to the problems of what to do with the children while she's in class, how to make her home and school schedules more compatible, how to afford tuition, and how to handle so many responsibilities at the same time; in essence, how to be a "superwoman."

A survey on the needs of older women students cited their most pressing problems as "time pressures, role definition, self-confidence, sense of direction, child care, and scheduling of courses" (Geisler and Thrush, 1975). The women also indicated a need for "vocational, educational, personal, and financial counseling and assistance with study skills and obtaining credit for life experience" (Geisler and Thrush, 1975).

Financial assistance may be a crucial factor in determining whether or not the mature woman can continue her education, and this is, of course, particularly true in the case of the low-income and minority-group women.

The scarcity of financial assistance for older women has not only curtailed the educational gains of these women, but has inhibited their professional development and mobility as well.

The reentry experience is not always a positive one. Some women maintain that, in attempting to schedule a return to school around obligations to home and family, they are accused of using the family as an excuse to avoid making a commitment. Writing about her experience with a continuing education program in New York, one woman stated:

> I began to realize that discontented middle-aged women constitute a lucrative clientele for a host of other women: psychologists, psychiatric social workers, career counselors. We were a gold mine. Those of us who had chosen to stay home were going to be advised, counseled, and exploited by women who had themselves rejected our lifestyle (Zanar, 1977, p. 85).

Women have the right to quality higher education; they are important resources to the nation. Mature women bring with them their life experience, which some colleges and universities are now accepting as partial credit for admission. Studies have also shown that mature women are more highly motivated to learn than younger students and do above average work (Fagin, 1971).

As policies and programs for continuing education change, so too does the older woman. The older woman of today will probably differ in many respects from the older woman of tomorrow. Their attitudes as well as their life styles are changing. More women are foregoing the option of marriage and/or children. What effects these decisions will have on continuing education programs is not yet discernible, but they are certain to have some effect (Geisler and Thrush, 1975).

One change that is already taking place is the ever-increasing number of older women enrolled in junior and community college programs. Continuing education programs at these locations should focus on how to best prepare these women to meet the needs of the neighboring communities (Taines, 1973), and also on how to adjust their programs to their new clientele.

The career possibilities of women are changing. Women no longer think only of being teachers or of entering the field of social work. More nontraditional programs are opening up in institutions of higher learning. The change is slow, but this is one aspect of continuing education that will be more noticeable in the future.

Although in existence for nearly two decades, continuing education for mature returning women is still fairly new. Its success depends on the success of its students, which in turn depends on the programs' having taken into account their uniqueness as a group of older women and as individuals, thereby enabling them to make worthwhile contributions to society.

ADJUSTMENT TO RETIREMENT

The issue of retirement adjustment of women has been neglected, partially because one theory of women's roles has postulated that because the role of wife and mother is the primary role for women, any type of work is temporary. Thus, women would be glad to leave the work role and return to their primary occupation.

While most older women did not train for paid employment, by the middle 1960s there were more women in their 40s in the labor force than women in their 20s and 30s. It would appear that retirement patterns for middle-aged women reflect the shift from the homemaker role to work role and that women who have ceased being homemakers would be reluctant to take up the role on retirement.

Of the many widely accepted stereotypes about women, one of the most pervasive and harmful is the belief that work is not meaningful to them. From this belief comes the rationalization that retirement is a minor event in the lives of working women. Expression of such stereotypes is widespread in retirement and gerontological literature. The view is largely based on role theory, which holds that giving up a primary role is what makes retirement a crisis. According to Palmore (1965), the worker role is more important to most men than to most women; for most women retirement does not mean giving up a primary role.

The woman retiree is often portrayed as having an advantage over the male retiree because she is imagined as returning to her primary role of wife and mother. In fact, women at retirement age are much less likely to be married than men (Ragan, 1977). In 1975 82 percent of the men aged 65 to 74 were married with spouse present, compared to only 67 percent of the women aged 65 to 74. Widowhood, of course, predominates among those women not married, with 42 percent of the 65- to 74-year-old women widowed (Siegel, 1976).

As a result of the traditional view that women's primary role is that of homemaker, special conflicts exist for many working women who must attempt to juggle successfully their multiple roles (Coyle and Fuller, 1977). Several studies (Coser and Rokoff, 1971; Sokolowska, 1965) view the problems of working women as resulting from the conflict between the dual roles of wife and worker. "Given the strain, for women workers, of combining demanding work and home obligations, one might expect women to be eager to retire" (Coyle and Fuller, 1977, p. 2).

But contradictory evidence exists about retirement attitudes. The data from the few empirical studies of the meaningfulness of work and the impact of retirement for women have shown the exact opposite of the stereotypes described earlier, suggesting the importance of work to women.

In a study of retired teachers and telephone company retirees (Atchley, 1976), respondents were asked to check from a list of life goals the areas in which failure would be most troublesome. Work was valued by most of the respondents; ". . . there were no significant sex differences in the importance of work" (Atchley, 1976, p. 208). This finding runs counter to the common assumption that work is less important as a life goal for women than it is for men.

Additionally, the retired men in this study were more likely to become accustomed to retirement in three months or less, a finding in opposition to the "commonsense pronouncements to the effect that retirement adjustment is easier among women because they have the housewife role to fall back on" (Atchley, 1976). Middle-class women seriously embrace work as a life goal and have more difficulty than men in giving up their jobs. Women are less likely than men to be positively oriented toward retirement (Jacobson, 1974) and more likely than men to express apprehension and display high anxiety about the effects of retirement (Atchley, 1976; Streib and Schneider, 1971).

Not only do women have a harder time getting used to retirement, they show a greater prevalence of negative psychological symptoms compared to retired men. Retired women are more often lonely, anxious, low in self-esteem and stability, highly sensitive to criticism, and highly depressed (Atchley, 1976). Males adjust to retirement faster than females, like retirement better, and have fewer negative psychological characteristics. Retirement does, then, constitute a crisis for today's older woman.

In addition to the psychological and social adjustments required of women when they retire, economic concerns often contribute to poor adjustment as well. The issues of social security and pensions are directly related to retirement and are of extreme importance to older women. Older women in America today constitute the single poorest group of people in our society (Kreps and Clark, 1975). More than 50 percent of all single women over the age of 65 live at or below the poverty level (which was defined as $3,400 annually by the U.S. Department of Labor on April 1, 1979). In 1975 only 5 percent of single women aged 65 and older were living on more than $5,000 annually. This is due in large part to the limitations of the social security and pension benefits available to middle-aged widows and to women over the age of 62.

Social Security

A number of social biases and inequities in the social security system contribute to the low socioeconomic status of older women on retirement. First, there is sex discrimination in employment. Social security benefits are based on earnings. Since women earn approximately half as much as men, their benefits are much lower on retirement.

Second, women are punished if they elect to drop out of the labor force to raise families. Benefits are calculated on average lifetime earnings. For every year a woman stays at home raising children, a zero gets averaged in, lowering her average lifetime earnings, and thus her social security benefits. In 1978 the average lifetime earnings were based on the highest salaried 22 years, a figure that will increase for each succeeding cohort until some maximum level is reached.

A third problem with social security benefits concerns the actuarial reduction. An individual may elect to receive benefits at age 62 instead of at age 65. Because benefits will be paid to the beneficiary for an additional three years, monthly benefits are smaller. Unfortunately, many women are in such financial binds as they age that they cannot wait the additional three years until age 65; they must begin collecting benefits at age 62. The reduced benefit helps maintain their impoverished status. In 1970 70 percent of the women did not hold out until age 65.

All wage earners pay into the social security system at the same rate. When more than one person in a family works, retirement income may be no greater than if only the husband paid into the system. A dependent wife with no earnings record of her own receives 50 percent of the amount of her husband's benefit when she is 65 (or 38 percent of the amount of his benefit when she is 62 if she elects to collect early).

A wife with her own earnings record may collect a benefit based on her own earnings or, as a dependent wife, on her husband's earnings record, whichever is greater. Thus, in many cases the employed wife receives no benefits for her payroll tax contributions.

Yet another inequity occurs for widows. Unless the widow is totally disabled and eligible for disability benefits, her widow's benefits cease when her youngest child turns 18. Her benefits resume at age 60. For many women widowed in their late 40s or early 50s, the several years that must elapse before help is forthcoming can be devastating. These women are generally not eligible for welfare, because one of the requirements is a housing payment that does not exceed $96 per month. Many widows are living in homes that require a greater monthly financial commitment than is allowed by welfare agencies and so cannot find help from that quarter. Too old to find jobs and too young for social security, these women have been called "displaced homemakers." Their plight is discussed in depth in Chapter 6. In cases of divorce, a woman married less than 10 years to her husband is ineligible for any benefits on his earnings record.

Despite so-called cost of living increases, social security payments have failed to keep up with the inflation of the 1970s. As rent, utilities, transportation, and other related expenses increase, many social security beneficiaries are forced to do without adequate food and medication.

Private Pensions

Historically, only one in five (20 percent) women retiring from jobs in private industry could expect to receive a pension, although one in two (50 percent) men could expect to receive a pension. Pensions for those women who do receive them are shockingly small; median benefits are approximately half of the median benefits paid to men. Survivors' benefits are uncommon; only 2 percent of all widows over 65 are receiving any benefit from their husband's pension plans (Blackwell and Ferguson, 1973). We will discuss later why this is so.

The private pension system covers only nongovernmental workers and includes some 44,000 *different* pension plans. These plans were virtually unregulated until 1976. Their provisions were varied, determined either by employers alone or through negotiations between employers and unions.

Approximately half the private labor force is not covered at all by the private pension system, and those who are covered are predominantly men. Nearly half of the employees who were covered by pension plans have never received the benefits to which they were entitled. Many of those employees are women.

Most women do not have savings or other assets to tide them over the 18 years that a woman is expected to live after age 65 (to age 83). Data collected by the U.S. Department of Labor (1977) indicate that 47 percent of women over age 65 live on less than $2,000 per year; 48 percent of women over age 65 live on $2,000 to $5,000 per year; and only 5 percent of women over age 65 live on more than $5,000 per year.

When women returned to work after raising children, many discovered that under some pension plans they were considered too old to enroll. Frequently, companies that hired large numbers of women, such as department stores, drug stores, and dime stores, had requirements that excluded new employees over age 45 from participation in the plan (Blackwell and Ferguson, 1973).

Pension plans are typically designed to benefit employees who stay many years in one job; usually that has meant male employees. Noncontinuous work often resulted in loss of pension benefits. Again, women more often than men were the ones to be laid off, since they tended to fill the more expendable positions, to take time out to raise children, or to work part-time. Because pension benefits are generally based on annual earnings during total years of continuous employment, women's pensions are smaller than men's.

For women who have worked outside the home all their lives earning good salaries, but have changed jobs several times, benefits are considerably smaller than a benefit from one employer would be. Some women may be unable to collect benefits at all if they have not stayed at each job for a specified number of years. Almost all plans have discriminated by paying lower monthly benefits to women because of their longer life expectancy, or by charging women more money than men for the same benefits. Other plans have established an earlier retirement age for women.

Pension plans were not designed to consider wives as equal partners. The pension benefit was considered to belong to only the employee, not to the wife. Many workers assumed their spouses would automatically get the pension after widowhood, a misconception that could not be remedied after the death of the pensioner. Some plans did have a survivor's benefit *option*. If the worker filed the right documents at the right time and agreed to take a substantially reduced pension in his own lifetime, his widow could receive a still smaller benefit after he died. Very few workers chose this option, as evidenced by the 2 percent of widows receiving any survivor's provisions (Blackwell and Ferguson, 1973).

If a worker, male or female, was not employed at retirement age, the pension could be lost. It was not uncommon practice to fire individuals a year before they retired. The pension contributions paid in over a lifetime were lost, and the workers had no recourse.

To prevent such questionable practices and to eliminate some of the more blatant discriminatory practices, Congress passed the Employee Retirement Income Security Act of 1974 (ERISA). The majority of the provisions of ERISA took effect in 1976, so pension protection has only been available for a very few years.

One of the major provisions of ERISA is directly relevant to widows. A pension plan that provides benefits in the form of an annuity must provide a participant and his or her spouse with a "joint and survivor annuity," unless the participant declines such protection for the spouse. The survivor's annuity must be no less than half of the joint annuity. It is important to note that when a pension participant elects this option, the monthly benefit will be smaller than it will be if the option is declined.

If the worker dies within ten years of retirement, his widow is still eligible for some benefits, if the worker has exercised his right to this protection. A wife is *not* informed if her husband declines to elect the survivor annuity; thus, it is important for wives to initiate inquiries as early in the pension progam as possible.

The law also prohibits an employer from discrimination between men and women on fringe and retirement benefits. Despite ERISA, discriminations still exist. The following case, presented to the Supreme Court, serves as an example.

Women with the Los Angeles Department of Water and Power claimed that the department practiced illegal sex discrimination because women were charged more than men for identical monthly pension benefits. A woman took home 15 percent less pay than a man with the same salary. The Department claimed they were not discriminating because women outlive men and thus will draw larger total sums in pension benefits than men. The Department claimed it was more generous to women because it matched each employee's pension payment with a 110 percent contribution of its own, and the women's matches were larger. Justices Warren Burger and William Rehnquist wondered aloud during the hearing if a decision that men and women must pay equally for pensions would entitle men to sue on the grounds that they were forced to subsidize higher total payments to women (Mintz, 1978).

This case has been decided in favor of the women. The United States Supreme Court held that "requiring men and women to make unequal contributions to an employer-operated pension fund violates Title VII of the Civil Rights Act of 1964" (*Academe*, 1978, p. 9). Such violations will probably be decided case-by-case, as suits are brought. Thus, the ERISA legislation is no guarantee that inequities for women in various pension plans have been eradicated.

SUMMARY

Women are returning to work in increasing numbers as male labor force participation is declining. Though popular stereotypes hold that work is unimportant to women, women are indicating that work is of great importance to them. The significance of work is emphasized by the reluctance of women to retire, and on retirement, to exhibit more negative psychological characteristics than retired men.

People are living longer than ever before, but retirement is not taking place significantly later in the life cycle. Therefore, the postretirement period keeps lengthening. Most women experience a longer postretirement period than do men since women live longer. Women often retire when their older husbands do, which is earlier than their own mandatory retirement age in many cases.

Economic limitations contribute to stress at retirement at the same time that social and psychological adjustments are required. Older women as a group are poor, since social security and pension benefits are often inadequate to cover the most basic needs.

■8
Ethnic and Racial Variations in Older Women

Older women in the United States are not a single group with common characteristics; rather they are individuals from a variety of ethnic and racial groups—Mexican Americans, Italian Americans, blacks, Jews, Asian Americans, Cubans, native Americans, Irish Americans, Polish Americans, Puerto Ricans, and many more. Many of these groups have experienced discrimination because of their minority status.

Each group has a distinctive subculture. Within the subculture, older age cohorts have experiences and characteristics that differ from the younger cohorts. Also, various ethnic and racial groups have differing cultural norms that influence their views about care for their aging members.

It is a complex task to weigh the significance of ethnicity as compared to other factors when analyzing various groups.

> . . . American ethnic groups differ in so many demographic, geographic, and other respects that it is necessary to separate out the effects of these other differences in order to determine how much effect ethnicity, as such, has on the behavior of ethnic groups themselves or on the larger society's behavior toward them (Sowell, 1978, p. 213).

The median age differences among ethnic groups are great. Americans of Irish or Italian ancestry have a median age of about 36 years, while the median age of those persons of Puerto Rican or Mexican origin is approximately 18 years. Russian Americans, who are mostly Jewish, have a median age of 45 years, nearly 2½ times older than the groups with the youngest median age. The median age differences influence the percentage of older women in a particular ethnic group. To illustrate, about 36 percent of Japanese-American women are aged 45 or over, while only 27 percent of Filipino-American women are in that age group.

Median age differences among groups also affect such age-related phenomena as fertility, income, and educational levels (Sowell, 1978). The fertility rate is influenced by the proportion of older women in a particular group. The older women tend to have had more children than the younger women because the older women have completed their families; the younger ones have not. However, older women reared children when larger families were the norm; younger women are not having as many children. Fertility rates and income levels are inversely related in American ethnic groups. The education levels of the older women in an ethnic group tend to be lower than those of the younger women.

> The magnitudes of the difference between age cohorts of the same ethnic group may be indicated by the fact that more than 20 percent of all blacks in the 55–65-year-old bracket, and more than 40 percent of all blacks, 65 and over, have less than five years of schooling, whereas less than 2 percent of blacks in the 25–29-year-old bracket had such little education (Sowell, 1978, p. 224).

The socioeconomic conditions of any ethnic group depends in part on where its members are located (Sowell, 1978). Immigrants who had little or no money left after their voyage to the United States usually settled in the ports of arrival. Blacks' locations were determined by the economic interests of the slave-holding South and later migratory patterns to seek jobs in the industrial cities of the North.

ETHNIC GROUPS COMPARED

Most research on ethnic and racial groups is not directed toward investigating sex or age differences within the group. More often studies compare one group with another and/or with the white majority. Thus, the information about various groups of women presented in this unit is gleaned mainly from sources providing general information about ethnic and racial groups. Black women, however, are an exception; researching focusing upon them as a separate group with special social and economic problems has begun in recent years.

Black and Hispanic females are more likely than white females to be the heads of households, forced to seek employment, encountering health problems, and living alone; they are less likely to have social support systems (Butler, 1978). In her random sample of Texas women 55 years of age and older, Blau and her associates (1978) reported a number of differences between Mexican-American, black, and Anglo women. The minority women perceived themselves to be "old" more often than Anglo women. They reported that their mental health was poorer. The black women had the fewest living children, while the Mexican-American women had the largest number. However, the black women were the most apt to have extensive informal social supports.

Older women who have minority status are less economically well off than white older women. For example, black and Hispanic women aged 65 and over had a lower median individual income than white women of similar ages. In addition, the median family incomes of black and Hispanic families with a female head are lower than for comparable white families. Since, as we have pointed out, older women are poor by any standard, the situation of black and Mexican-American women is a national disgrace.

Families headed by minority women are of special concern because of the great incidence of poverty among them. "In 1977, one out of every nine white families was headed by a woman as compared with one of every three black families and one of every five Mexican-American families" (Blau et al., 1978, p. 70). One factor contributing to the low economic status is the higher jobless rate of minority women heading families. Such black women are twice as likely to be unemployed as whites, while Mexican-American women heads of families have a rate of unemployment nearly as high as their black counterparts.

A lower level of education also contributes to the poverty in families headed by women. In 1978 the U.S. Labor Department reported that one out of five female heads of families had not even attended high school (Blau et al., 1978). Age and minority status are related to even lower educational attainment. Three-fourths of all black women 45 years and older who head families have not completed high school; 74 percent of *all* Mexican-American women family heads had not finished high school (Johnson,

1978). Lower educational attainment is related to higher fertility rates and lower labor force participation rates. "Today each additional child diminishes the woman's prospects for economic independence and security through employment, and increases her chances of poverty" (Blau et al., 1978, p. 3).

Even if minority women are able to find jobs, the type of work, career patterns, and retirement benefits create less economic security than for white women. "Minority women are less likely to work for employers who have retirement benefits; they are more likely to experience health-related early retirement; they are more likely to retire following unemployment; they are more likely to have had 'disorderly' work careers that generate low earnings, low social security, and no pension" (Atchley, 1978).

Four factors—old age, inadequate income, minority status, and female gender—build on each other to create life situations with increasing possibilities for loss and injury. To be old puts a person in jeopardy in our society; to be old and poor equals double jeopardy; to be old, poor, and a minority creates triple jeopardy; and to be old, poor, a minority, and female equals quadruple jeopardy (Perry, 1978).

Hispanic Women

According to 1975 census figures, the total Hispanic population is 11.2 million (Butler and Lewis, 1977). This includes people from Cuba, Central and South America, Mexico, Puerto Rico, and other Spanish people. The Mexican Americans are the largest subgroup—6 to 7 million. Eighty percent of the Mexican Americans live in urban areas, primarily in five southwestern states: Arizona, California, Colorado, New Mexico, and Texas (Butler and Lewis, 1977). People aged 65 and over make up only 4 percent of the Spanish-American population as compared with 10 percent of the white population because the median age is lower. (An exception is the Cuban population, with 8.6 percent 65 and over).

Most Hispanic women are married rather than widowed, divorced, or separated. Mexican-American women generally go on bearing children at a much later age than Anglo women (Moore, 1971). Traditional patterns of decision-making and division of household tasks are likely to be a part of the older Hispanic woman's life. The older woman has been viewed as the pillar of the family.

Mexican-American women family heads have the lowest rate of participation in the labor force, as compared with white and black female family heads (Blau et al., 1978). Having many small children in the home is a major deterrent to working. A lower educational level, which discourages the learning of English, and illegal immigrant status are other barriers to participation in the labor force.

Rural older Hispanic women consider their role in the extended family important for advising their children and others and for acquainting the younger generations with Spanish history and tradition (Streib, 1976). However, extended family care is a myth for the majority of those of Hispanic origin (Estrada, 1977). The proportion of Hispanic elderly living with their children is approximately 10 percent, with a slightly higher proportion in rural areas. Hispanic women are three times more likely to live alone than in someone else's home.

In a study by Bremer and Ragan (1977), the Mexican-American women who lived in homes with their children and grandchildren more often reported feeling less useful as they grew older than did the women who lived with no children under 18. The researchers suggested that factors such as poverty, a low level of education, widowhood, and loss of independence detracted from their happiness. Generational differences within the subculture may have been an additional factor.

Jewish Women

People aged 65 and over comprise 12 percent of the Jewish community as of 1971 (Council of Jewish Federations, n.d.). Of these older people, women exceed men, 56 percent women to 44 percent men. Only 7 percent of Jewish households contain three generations. Over 40 percent of households are one-person households, due mainly to widowhood, but also to separation and divorce. Thirty-five percent of Jewish women aged 65 and over are heads of households.

American-Indian Women

Nearly 89,000 American Indians aged 55 and over live in the United States on and off reservations (U.S. DHEW, 1977). Fewer than 40,000 are aged 65 and over; this is less than 5 percent of the total American-Indian population as compared to 6 percent for blacks and 10 percent for whites in that age bracket (Institute of Gerontology, 1971). The smaller percentage of old American Indians is due to their shorter life expectancy; their average life expectancy is approximately 45 years. American-Indian women tend to live longer than American-Indian men. Fifty-five of each 100 American Indians reaching age 65 are women.

American Indians are the poorest people in the United States, and older Indians are even poorer than younger Indians. In 1971 one-half of the Indian families had yearly incomes of less than $4,000 (Butler and Lewis, 1977). Traditional extended family help is not possible if the family itself has no resources.

Anglo Ethnic Women

The experience of white ethnics is largely unexplored by gerontologists (Fandetti and Gelfand, 1976). Yet 9 million European immigrants have entered the United States since 1940, and the proportion of aged in these ethnic communities continues to grow. Although there has been some modification of values and life styles, especially for second- and third-generation members, the extended family network continues to play a central role in helping individual members deal with problems (Fandetti and Gelfand, 1978).

The 55 to 65-year-old family members, especially the women, may be the care providers for their aging parents as well as for their own children. Families in some white ethnic groups are willing to consider using long-term care facilities, but only for elderly relatives needing intensive medical care.

East Asian-American Women

Two million East Asian Americans (primarily Chinese, Filipino, Japanese, Korean, and Samoan) make up about 1 percent of the United States population (Butler and Lewis, 1977). The majority live in metropolitan areas of California and Hawaii. Pre-World War II immigration policies forced disruption of normal Chinese family life, prohibiting Chinese women and children from accompanying the men to the United States. Thus, elderly Chinese-American males outnumber females. Japanese Americans did not suffer the severe immigration restrictions that affected Chinese-American family life. However, one-fifth of the Japanese-American elderly are poor. Most (81 percent) of the Filipino-American population is male, due to historical patterns of immigration; 30 percent of these men have interracial marriages.

Black Women

About 25 percent of black women are 45 years or older. There were 3.1 million black women in this age category in 1974. Increases to 3.6 million black women 45 years and older by 1984 and 4.4 million such women by 1994 are expected (Jackson, 1975-76). The life expectancy of a black woman

40 years old in 1970 is 73.8 years compared with 78.1 years for a white woman of the same age (U.S. Depart. Commerce, 1977a). The mortality rate of black women 45 to 64 years of age is approximately twice that of white women in the same age range (Perry, 1978). However, according to 1973 census figures, a black woman reaching age 60 can expect to live to age 79, only 1.7 years less than a white woman who reaches age 60.

Sixty-one percent of the black elderly aged 65 years and over still live in the South; the rest are fairly evenly divided between the Northeast and North Central regions, with only 5 percent in the West (Institute of Gerontology, 1971). In the South, the movement of younger blacks to northern cities has left a disproportionate number of older blacks in non-metropolitan areas.

Much of the information about the lives of married blacks has been based on limited impressions by untrained observers. Recent research has challenged the myth of the matriarchal pattern as the dominant one in black families. In her study of the marital life of low-income older blacks living in a Southern urban area, Jacquelyne Jackson (1972b) found that the wife was not the dominant spouse when there were major decisions to be made about money and economic security, illness, and child-rearing. "Spouse dominance tends to vary according to the specific areas of decision-making, with wives having more influence within areas traditionally relegated to them . . ." (Jackson, 1972b, p. 26).

Older black couples in the above study did not engage in many joint activities. Attending church together, visiting, relatives, and shopping were the most frequent shared activities. The wives performed the family jobs that were traditionally considered feminine: cooking, cleaning, washing, and ironing; while the males appeared more involved in masculine tasks such as yard work and home repairs.

A study of married and spouseless (single, divorced, or widowed) black women revealed that their lives are similar in some respects (Jackson, 1972a). Both groups have more contact and satisfaction with friends than with their children. However, the spouseless women were much more likely to spend time outside the home with friends, while the married women more often visited relatives. Both groups of women reported their most frequent activities with their children were spending holidays, vacations, and brief visits together.

Social-class differences among black women affect the amount of their leisure-time activities (Lambing, 1972). The upper-middle-class women had twice as many leisure interests on the average as the upper-lower-class women and three times as many as the lower-lower-class women. Upper-class black women averaged between three and four memberships in voluntary organizations as compared to slightly more than two for upper-lower-class women and just under one for lower-lower-class women. Many of the lower-lower-class women had to give up membership because of limited finances. Black women who lived in segregated urban public housing usually carried out their activities alone (Ehrlich, 1973). Thus, the crucial factor of low income contributes to creating isolation.

Because of the shorter life expectancy of black men as compared to white men, black women experience widowhood earlier in life and have higher widowhood rates. Especially among black women who are 65 years or older, marriage is not the dominant pattern. "In 1970, about two-thirds of these aged black females were widows, and were, of course, more likely to be widowed than were white females (54 percent) of the same ages" (Jackson, 1972b, p. 27). As in the past, it appears that the older black widows still depend on their families for support; however, many have no living children and must reach out to secondary kin such as siblings, cousins, and even "make-believe" kin (Jackson, 1972a).

There is contradictory evidence on the involvement of older black women in extended-family networks. Elderly black couples are more likely than elderly white couples to have grandchildren, nieces, and nephews under 18 living in their homes (Institute of Gerontology, 1971). Fourteen percent of elderly black couples take in children of relatives as compared with 3 percent of elderly white couples. Almost half of the black families headed by an older woman (48 percent) have relatives' children living with them as contrasted with only 10 percent of comparable white families. These black grandparents serve as a point of anchorage and provide supports for their grandchildren that cannot be given by the the parents (Jackson, 1975).

Historically, the black grandmother has been perceived as a source of love, strength, and stability in the black family. "No matter what social and economical conditions the black family has faced, the black grandmother has been a steady, supporting influence, as well as a connecting link between branches of the extended family" (Jones, 1972, p. 19). She had learned how to deal with the dominant white society and survive. She was an authority on having babies and caring for them, curing common illnesses, and preparing tasty meals from little food. She stressed independence and self-reliance as aids in coping with the hostile outside world. She emphasized cooperation as a means of helping her family survive and grow.

The influence of the black grandmother has been reduced as black families migrated to urban areas and adopted middle-class values and life styles. "Today the black grandmother often lives in, and maintains, the family home, where children and grandchildren gather during the summer or at Christmas to renew, maintain, and strengthen family ties. Family members who suffer temporary set backs also use this family home as a refuge" (Jones, 1972, p. 21). Some data about grandparenting suggest that many black grandparents who have grandchildren living in their homes would prefer to live independently (Jackson, 1972b). However, the circumstances, such as outside employment of the parents of the child, create a feeling of obligation to extend help.

In her study of black widows living in an urban area, Lopata (1975b) found that the common assumption that older black widows live rich and full lives surrounded by kin was not true. Two-thirds of the black widows had no children in the home, had little or no contact with siblings, and belonged to no organizations. Three-fifths were not church members. Their social relationships were similar to those of older white widows. Thus, they were just as isolated as white widows.

Hobart Jackson (1978), the founder of the National Caucus on the Black Aged, asserts that the extended family that assured a home for the mother, grandmother, or maiden aunt no longer exists as a predominant way of life. He sees older women more often living in a room or an apartment, on an insufficient income and in fear of their surroundings, and often becoming lonely and alienated.

Older black women generally have unfavorable housing conditions. In 1970 in regions outside the South, about 30 percent of those 55 to 64 years of age, 34 percent of those 65 to 74 years of age, and 40 percent of those 75 years and over still lived in homes without all plumbing facilities, for example, hot and cold running water, indoor flush toilet, and bathtub or shower (Jackson, 1975-76).

The majority of older black women live in poverty. Forty-seven percent of black women aged 65 and over had under $1,000 in annual income in 1969 (Perry, 1978). Median income for elderly black couples was $3,222 in 1969 as compared with $4,884 for whites. The number of black women who are the main wage earners for their families increases with age.

Income often barely covers the cost of consumption items alone; yet since many older black women still work, they have transportation and other work-related expenses. Twelve percent of black women over 65 years of age continue to be part of the labor force. Twenty-six percent of married black women over age 65 remain in the labor force, while only 15 percent of elderly white wives continue employment (Institute of Gerontology, 1971).

Older black women frequently have jobs with long hours and poor working conditions. A majority (55 percent) of older black women are private household workers; 20 percent are nonhousehold service workers (Atchley, 1978). "The black woman comes to old age physically and mentally exhausted, with few economic or social resources upon which to draw" (Jackson, 1978, p. 19).

SUMMARY

Older minority women in the United States cannot be described as a group with common characteristics other than the fact that they are more likely to live in situations of poverty than older white women. Six minority groups are described in some detail: Hispanic, Jewish, American Indian, Anglo ethnic, East Asian American, and black. Each group has its unique characteristics.

The majority of Hispanic women are married rather than widowed, divorced, or single. Decision-making and division of household tasks are frequently carried out within traditional male-female patterns. Extended family involvement and care are somewhat more frequent for Hispanic women in rural areas than for those in urban areas.

Information concerning the life situations of Jewish, American-Indian, and East Asian-American older women is in the form of isolated facts; no overall picture is available. Forty percent of older Jewish women, most of whom are widows, live in one-person households. American-Indian women tend to live longer than American-Indian men; however, the average life expectancy is only approximately 45 years. There are more elderly Chinese-American males than females because of pre-World War II immigration restrictions that prevented Chinese women and children from accompanying the men to the United States. Japanese Americans did not suffer the same restrictions that affected Chinese-American family life.

Gerontologists have given little attention to the experiences of older women and men in white ethnic groups, even though the proportion of older people continues to grow. The extended family usually plays a central role in providing support to individual members. The 55- to 65-year-old family members, especially women, may care for their aging parents as well as their own children.

Black women 45 years and older comprise about 25 percent of all black women. Due to the shorter life expectancy of black men as compared to white men, black women become widows earlier in life and are more likely to be widowed than white women. Older black women generally have unfavorable housing conditions. Their jobs frequently entail long hours, poor working conditions, and low income. There is contradictory evidence about whether black women gain support from their extended family networks or are isolated or depend on friends for companionship.

■9
Research Issues

It should be readily apparent that gerontological literature has not focused to a large degree on the female aging process. This neglect is a direct reflection of the paucity of research efforts currently directed toward resolving the numerous questions that can be raised about the physiological, psychological, and sociological changes that occur during a woman's middle and later years. The purpose of this chapter is not to resolve these many issues. Such resolution will require research efforts from many disciplines, particularly sociology, psychology, economics, and health. Rather, this chapter poses a number of research questions. Some will have become obvious to the reader by now; others are more subtle, but important nonetheless. As these questions are explored, new questions will arise. Only through intensive multidisciplinary research efforts can existing gaps in the literature be reduced and a better understanding of the female aging process be reached.

DEMOGRAPHIC DATA

Population information complied through census surveys allows the researcher to employ secondary data analysis techniques on a national scale. Despite the availability of such statistics, little work has focused on characteristics of the older female population. Demographic trends can provide insight about future cohorts of the elderly female population. As more and more women live an increasing number of years, it is crucial to establish what demands will be placed on communities for social services, housing, transportation, and other related issues. In addition to needs assessment, public policy alternatives should be evaluated in order to determine how to best meet established needs.

IMAGES OF OLDER WOMEN

Myths and stereotypes generally reflect cultural mores. Examination of cultural bias is a first step toward breaking down existing barriers. Only through a clear understanding of myth and reality can researchers attempt to reduce negative views and improve attitudes toward older women. Because the mass media mirror cultural beliefs, numerous research efforts have determined in what ways media portrayals of middle-aged and older women are inaccurate. The next needed step lies in establishing how much the various media forms influence behavior and how such influence might be used in a positive way.

MENOPAUSE AND SEXUALITY

Cultural biases describe menopause as an affliction, and many women and physicians do not consider it a normal physiological change. What social judgments are made and *why* they are made about a biological change is an important research issue. Of greater importance, perhaps, are the psychological issues that emerge for women as a result of social judgments. The prescribing of estrogen for menopausal women remains controversial. Research must continue to focus on efforts to determine the true relationship between estrogen and cancer. It is clear that much additional data are needed, specifically systematic knowledge of the natural course of menopause without estrogen replacement therapy (ERT), as well as the optimal way to provide ERT where required. Artificial menopause, or hysterectomy, is a related issue that continues to require investigation. The number of such operations performed yearly suggests that closer scrutiny of the medical profession is warranted.

Social attitudes create strong disapproval for a sexual role for older women. Research in this area should not be limited to physiological sexual response mechanisms. Of equal importance is a clear understanding of attitudes about sexuality. How attitudes are developed, maintained, and possibly altered is an area seldom touched on in major studies of sexuality. A related issue involves the societal attitudes toward women who have had a mastectomy. How is the adjustment of a woman who has undergone this form of surgery affected by societal attitudes? A woman who believes that sexuality is inappropriate at an advanced age may have a very different psychological reaction to the loss of a breast than a woman who accepts sexuality as part of the aging process.

MENTAL HEALTH

The subject of the mental health and emotional well-being of middle-aged and older women is one largely untouched by the research community. Variance in suicide rates, visits to physicians, and use of psychotropic drugs suggest that the mental health needs of older women differ from those of older men. A number of questions can be raised.

- how do the adjustments faced by older women affect their mental health?
- how is stress related to changes in an older woman's life?
- what physical and social changes contribute to depression in women?
- do older men experience similar changes and similar depressions?
- what factors contribute to the suicide rate of middle-aged and older women?

LIFE SITUATIONS

A popular view of the female aging process suggests that women have an easy transition to old age because aging for them begins earlier and lasts longer than it does for men. The justification for this view evolves out of role theory, which suggests that the role of widow is an honored one and that younger married women may be frustrated because they are not eligible to join that ready-made peer group. Certainly no empirical data support such a notion.

A number of issues related to life situations must be considered if older women's roles are to be more fully understood. The factors that appear to force women to make changes in their roles as they age are understood only in a superficial way. How do such changes promote or detract from the life statisfaction of older women of varying characteristics and life styles? In the same vein, data concerning the limitations and fulfillments within the roles that older women now have would make such women more visible and counteract the tendency to see older women as members of a group with common characteristics.

Living arrangements and social contacts have much influence on the life style of older women. Why are increasing numbers of older women living alone, and what makes this a satisfactory or unsatisfactory situation? What are the crucial factors that influence the kind and quality of social networks of older women? How does moving to a more age-segregated setting, such as a retirement community, nursing home, or apartment building for older people affect social contacts? Focus on determining the quality and variety within women's life situations will move policy-making and program development beyond reliance on stereotypes and demographic data.

FAMILY RELATIONS

Widowhood has been one of the few areas in which major research has been conducted. No less important, but less frequently examined, are other family issues with direct impact on the older women.

For years, the "empty nest" period was touted as a major transition for the middle-aged woman. More recently, evidence suggests that a child's leaving home may not induce feelings of uselessness in older women. The "empty nest" may be filled by aging parents who require assistance from their adult children. Little work has been done to assess how such a responsibility affects the women who have to provide such assistance or what the stresses are on the aging woman who must live with her children.

Studies of the marriage relationship of older couples do not provide consistent information about the quality of these relationships. The positive and negative factors affecting couples in long-term marriages, as well as those couples who have remarried, are little understood. What do couples value in the marital relationship in later life? Does the marital relationship undergo change when a husband retires?

The maintenance of family relationships traditionally has fallen within the woman's domain. Perceived social expectations may cloud the actual importance of family relationships to older women. Contacts with spouse, grandchildren, adult children, siblings, and other relatives may vary in importance over the life span rather than being constant. The meaningfulness of these contacts in the eyes of older women of various ages needs to be given more attention.

EMPLOYMENT AND RETIREMENT

Demographic data indicate very clearly that labor force participation by older women has changed dramatically during the past 20 years. Disparities in wages earned by similarly aged men and women are also easy to document. Most research on women and work has neglected the underlying social and psychological factors that have influenced shifts in labor force participation and wage levels. Where such exploratory efforts have been attempted, subjects have usually been younger women, typically aged 35 or less. Thus, we have relatively limited knowledge of why older women return to work and whether their work is as meaningful to them as it is to men.

A closely related issue, retirement, is similarly unexplored. The literature is unable to identify what retirement is like for older women. Effective preretirement programs require an understanding of whether women's adjustment to retirement is more or less difficult than men's adjustment. While factors strongly related to male satisfaction with retirement have been identified in numerous studies, it has yet to be determined what factors correlate to retirement satisfaction for women.

ETHNIC AND RACIAL VARIATIONS IN OLDER WOMEN

Studies concerning ethnic and racial variations among women of any age are rare. Ethnic and nonwhite populations are frequently eliminated from studies for various reasons, such as insignificant numbers within the sample or the creation of confounding variables within a research design. Thus, research issues in this area are largely unexplored; all of the dimensions mentioned in the previous sections could be used to create much-needed data. Even a quantitative picture of the lives of older ethnic and nonwhite older women based on demographic data has yet to be drawn.

SUMMARY

Future research must promote an understanding of individual women as they carry on their lives at various ages and points in history.

> Many changes are occurring among women at the present time. But we must be cautious in accepting without question, the mass media's version of what is happening. Our study of the commitments of women to work and family roles indicate no sudden changes, but rather more individualistic combinations of roles during the life course (Lopata, 1978, p. 49).

The impact of major events, such as the two World Wars and the Great Depression, and various social trends, such as the feminist movement, on successive cohorts of women needs to be studied in depth. There are significant differences in the lives of women born at various points in history. Neugarten and Brown-Rezanka (1978) compared three groups of women, one group aged 60 to 65 in 1975, a second group aged 40 to 45 in 1975, and a third group aged 25 to 30 in 1975. The majority of women who are now 60 to 65 were born into big families and had at least one foreign-born parent. Only half of these women finished high school and very few finished college. Because of the Depression, a sizable proportion remained childless, and the overall birthrate of this group was the lowest recorded up to that time. The women in the 40 to 45 age group were born during the Depression and so were raised in small families. The majority finished high school, but few finished college. They married early and had relatively large families. More of this group has been or will be divorced than in the older group, but fewer will have been widowed by age 60. They will have more children to turn to in their old age than the women in the older age group. The youngest group of women were reared in large families and have higher educational and occupational levels. The majority plan to have only one or two children, and so they will have more child-free years within their life span than the other two groups of women.

How do women of *various* cohorts describe their lives today, and how have their lives evolved over time? Of equal consideration is the increasing variability *within* a particular cohort of women as they age. Women become more different with the passage of time as choices and commitments create unique life patterns, and interests and activities become more individualized (Neugarten and Brown-Rezanka, 1978). The options for health care, community activities, living arrangements, work, recreation, and education need to be broad in scope to meet the needs of women over their extended life span.

There are many more areas to dealing with loss than widowhood and retirement, and they must be explored. The social value of particular roles for women has changed substantially. Technological advances create the need for information-processing and skill-building at ever-increasing rates. These changes create many types of loss that women must handle on both a practical and an emotional level.

How can older women integrate the past with the present and remain whole human beings rather than people who downgrade and discredit what they have been and focus only on coping with present-day demands and expectations for the future. Examination of the common history of women within this century would assist women in the integration task just described. In particular, what are the positive threads that link young, middle-aged, old, and very old women? Much has been written about what has been detrimental to women's lives in the past. Uncovering such links would provide a more complete picture of women; of their common heritage and sources of strength in their individual lives.

There is an immediate need for research studies that provide the basis for the creation of policies that link older women with existing resources for social involvement. Many women, both middle-aged and older, are unable to take the information they gain from the mass media and put it to use. Society can do much more to assist women in replacing the supports that they automatically expect to have in their lives as they grow older but that in actuality are not available. The overall goal of research about older women must be to inspire policies and programs with a great deal of flexibility to accommodate the increasing size and heterogeneity of the aging female population.

Bibliography

Abdo, E., Dills, J., Shectman, H., and Yanish, M. Elderly women in institutions versus those in public housing: comparison of personal and social adjustments. *Journal of the American Geriatrics Society*, 1973, *21*(2), 81–87.

Abrahams, R. B. Mutual help for the widowed. *Social Work*, 1972, *17*(5), 54–61.

Academe. A report: Supreme Court decides Manhart. 1978, *12*(2), 9–11.

Alexander, S. *Shana Alexander's State-by-State Guide to Women's Legal Rights*. Los Angeles: Wollstonecraft, 1975.

Alvarez, W. C. Osteoporosis: a disease that attacks millions. *Geriatrics*, 1970, *25*(7), 77–78.

———. Trends in the social habits of elderly Americans. *Geriatrics*, 1972, *27*(2), 77.

Amundsen, K. *The Silenced Majority: Women and American Democracy*. Englewood Cliffs: Prentice-Hall, 1971.

Antunes, C., Stolley, P. D., Rosenshein, N. B., Davies, J. L., Tonascia, J. A., Brown, C., Burnett, L., Rutledge, A., Pokempner, M., and Garcia, R. Endometrial cancer and estrogen use: report of a large case-control study. *New England Journal of Medicine*, 1979, *300*(1), 9–13.

Arens, D. A. Widowhood and well-being: an interpretation of sex differences. Paper presented at the annual meeting of the Gerontological Society (Washington, D.C., Nov. 1979).

Arling, G. Resistance to isolation among elderly widows. *International Journal of Aging and Human Development*, 1976, *7*(1), 67–84.

Armstrong, J. B. Overmedicated society? *Canadian Medical Association Journal*, 1975, *112*(4), 413.

Atchley, R. C. Age and suicide in the United States. Oxford, Ohio: Scripps Foundation Gerontological Center, 1974.

——. Dimensions of widowhood in later life. *Gerontologist*, 1975, *15*(2), 176–178.

——. Selected social and psychological differences between men and women in later life. *Journal of Gerontology*, 1976, *31*(2), 204–211.

——. Retirement preparation for women. In A. F. Cahn (ed.), *Women in Midlife—Security and Fulfillment (part I)*. Washington, D.C.: GPO, 1978.

Ballard, L. A. Gynecologic surgery in the aged. *Geriatrics*, 1969, *24*(4), 172–178.

Bart, P. Why women's status changes in middle age: the turns of the social ferris wheel. *Sociological Symposium*, 1969, *3*, 1–18.

Bean, P. Accidental and intentional self-poisoning in the over sixty age group. *Gerontologicas Clinica*, 1973, *15*, 259–267.

Beeson, D. Women in studies of aging: a critique and suggestion. *Social Problems*, 1975, *23*(1), 52–59.

Bell, P. The double standard. *Trans-Action*, 1970, *8*, 75–80.

Bender, A. D., Geriatric pharmacology: Age and its influence on drug action in adults. *Drug Information Bulletin*, 1970, *3*, 153–158.

Bengtson, V. L., Kasschau, L., and Ragan, P. K. The impact of social structure on aging individuals. In J. E. Birren and K. W. Schaie (eds.), *Handbook of the Psychology of Aging*. New York: Van Nostrand Reinhold, 1977.

Bennett, A. E. Psychiatric management of geriatric depressive disorders. *Diseases of the Nervous System*, 1973, *34*(5), 222–225.

Benson, R. A., and Brodie, D. C. Suicide by overdoses of medicines among the aged. *Journal of the American Geriatrics Society*, 1975, *23*(7), 304–308.

Berardo, F. Survivorship and social isolation: the case of the aged widower. *The Family Coordinator*, 1970, *19*(1), 11–15.

Bergquist, L. Recycling lives. *Ms.*, 1973, *2*(2), 58–61+.

Bernard, J. Homosociality and female depression. *Journal of Social Issues*, 1976, *32*(4), 213–237.

Blackman, D., Howe, M., and Pinkston, W. M. Increasing participation in social interaction of the institutionalized elderly. *Gerontologist*, 1976, *16*(1, part I).

Blackwell, K., and Ferguson, K. Pensions: are there holes in your security blanket? *Ms.*, 1973, *2*(4), 14–18.

Blau, Z. Changes in status and age identification. *American Sociological Review*, 1956, *21*(2), 198–203.

——. *Old age in a changing society*. New York: Franklin Watts, 1973.

Blau, Z. S. Structural constraints on friendships in old age. *American Sociological Review*, 1961, *26*(3), 429–439.

——, Rogers, P. O., Oster, G. T., and Stephenson, R. C. School bells and work whistles: sounds that echo a better life for women in later years. In A. F. Cahn (ed.), *Women in Midlife—Security and Fulfillment (part 1)*. Washington, D.C.: GPO, 1978.

Blauner, R. Death and social structure. In B. L. Neugarten (ed.), *Middle Age and Aging*. Chicago: University of Chicago Press, 1968.

Bock, E. W., and Webber, I. L. Suicide among the elderly: isolating widowhood and mitigating alternatives. *Journal of Marriage and the Family*, 1972, *34*(1), 24–31.

Borgman, D. Medication abuse by middle-aged women. *Social Casework*, 1973, *54*(9), 526–532.

Boston Women's Health Book Collective. *Our Bodies, Ourselves*. Rev. ed. New York: Simon and Schuster, 1976.

Bourne, P. G. Drug abuse in the aging. *Perspective on Aging*, 1973, *2*, 18–20.

Brand, F., and Smith, R. Life adjustment and relocation of the elderly. *Journal of Gerontology*, 1974, *29*(3), 336–340.

Bremer, T. H., and Ragan, P. K. The effect of the empty nest on the morale of Mexican American and white women. Paper presented at the 30th annual meeting of the Gerontological Society. (San Francisco, Nov. 1977).

Brody, E. M. Congregate care facilities and mental health of the elderly. *Aging and Human Development*, 1970, *1*(4), 279–321.

———. *A Social Work Guide for Long-Term Care Facilities*. Rockville, Md.: National Institute of Mental Health, 1974.

Brown, C. L. Ageism and the women's movement. In J. R. Leppaluato et al. (eds.), *Women on the Move*. Eugene, Ore.: University of Oregon, 1973.

Burr, W. R. Satisfaction with various aspects of marriage over the life cycle: a random middle-class sample. *Journal of Marriage and the Family*, 1970, *32*, 29–37.

Burrows, G., and Harari, E. Psychiatric aspects of drug overdose in adults. *Anaesthesia and Intensive Care*, 1974, *2*(4), 310–315.

Butler, R. N. *Why Survive? Being Old in America*. New York: Harper and Row, 1975.

———. Prospects for middle-aged women. In A. F. Cahn (ed.), *Women in Midlife—Security and Fulfillment (part 1)*. Washington, D.C.: PO, 1978.

———, and Lewis, M. *Aging and Mental Health: Postivie Psychosocial Approaches*. St. Louis: C. V. Mosby, 1973; revised, 1977.

Caine, L. *Widow*. New York: William Morrow, 1974.

———. *Lifelines*. New York: William Morrow, 1978.

Carp, F. M. Housing and living environments of older people. In R. H. Binstock and E. Shanas (eds.), *Handbook of Aging and the Social Sciences*. New York: Van Nostrand Reinhold, 1976.

Cavan, R. Self and role in adjustment during old age. In J. Heiss (ed.), *Family Roles and Interaction*. Chicago: Rand McNally, 1968.

Chambers, C. D., and Griffey, M. Use of legal substances within the general population: the sex and age variables. *Addictive Diseases,* 1975, *2*(1-2), 7–19.

Clark, A. N. G., and Mankikar, C. B., and Gray, I. Gross self-neglect late in life may be a reaction to stress. *Lancet,* 1975, *1,* 366–368.

Clark, M., and Anderson, B. *Culture and Aging.* Springfield, Ill.: Charles C Thomas, 1967.

Claven, S., and Vatter, E. The affiliated family: a device for integrating old and young. *Gerontologist,* 1972, *12,* 407–412.

Clayton, P. J., Halikas, J. A., and Maurice, W. L. The depression of widowhood. *British Journal of Psychiatry,* 1972, *120,* 71–77.

Collins, M. Pioneering the future. *Prime Time,* 1976, *5*(6), 4–7.

Corea, G. Member tackles pro-estrogen M. D. *National Women's Health Collective Network News,* 1978, Apr.-May, 14.

Coser, R. L., and Rokoff, G. Women in the occupational world: social disruption and conflict. *Social Problems,* 1971, *18*(4), 535–554.

Council of Jewish Federations and Welfare Funds. *The Jewish Aging: Facts for Planning.* New York: Council for Jewish Federations and Welfare Funds, n.d.

Coyle, J. M., and Fuller, M. M. Women's work and retirement attitudes. Paper presented at the 30th annual meeting of the Gerontological Society (San Francisco, Nov. 1977).

Craddick, R. A., Leipold, V., and Leipold, W. D. Effect of role empathy on human figures drawn by women alcoholics. *Journal of Studies on Alcohol,* 1976, *37*(1), 90–97.

Craig, T. J., Comstock, G. W., and Geiser, P. B. Epidemiological comparison of breast cancer patients with early and late onset of malignancy and general population controls. *Journal of the National Cancer Institute,* 1974, *53*(6), 1577–1581.

Derx, E. I. Recreational activity for institutionalized children or adults. *Journal of Psychiatric Nursing and Mental Health Service,* 1972, *10*(6), 12–14.

Deutscher, I. The quality of postparental life. In B. L. Neugarten (ed.), *Middle Age and Aging.* Chicago: University of Chicago Press, 1968.

———. From parental to post-parental life: exploring shifting expectations. *Sociological Symposium,* 1969, *3,* 47–60.

Dressler, D. M. Life adjustment of retired couples. *International Journal of Aging and Human Development,* 1973, *4*(4), 335–349.

Durlak, J. A. Relationship between attitude toward life and death among elderly women. Developmental Psychology, 1973, *8*(1), 146.

Ehrlich, Ira F. Toward a social profile of the aged black population in the United States: an exploratory study. *International Journal of Aging and Human Development,* 1973, *4*(3), 271–276.

Ernst, M. *Self-esteem among Older Institutionalized Females*. Dallas, Tex.: Dallas Geriatric Research Institute, 1974.

Estrada, L. The Spanish origin elderly: a demographic survey 1970–1975. *Aging Research Utilization Report*, 1977, *4*(1), 13–14.

Fagin, M. D. Analysis of the performance of adult women in Missouri on three general examinations of the college level Examination Program. *Adult Education*, 1971, *21*(3), 148–165.

Fandetti, D. V., and Gelfand, D. E. Care of the aged: attitudes of white ethnic families. *Gerontologist*, 1976, *16*(6), 544–549.

————. Attitudes toward symptoms and services in the ethnic family and neighborhood. *American Journal of Orthopsychiatry*, 1978, *48*(3), 477–486.

Faulkner, A. O., Heisel, M. A., and Simms, P. Life strengths and life stresses: explorations in the measurement of the mental health of the black aged. *American Journal of Orthopsychiatry*, 1975, *45*(1), 102–110.

Fengler, A. P. Attitudinal orientations of wives toward their husbands' retirement. *International Journal of Aging and Human Development*, 1975, *6*, 139–152.

Friedman, M. and Rosenman, R. H. *Type A Behavior and Your Heart*. New York: Knopf, 1974.

Gaitz, C. M. and Scott, J. Analysis of letters to "Dear Abby" concerning old age. *Gerontologist*, 1975, *15*(1), 47–50.

Garai, J. E. Sex differences in mental health. *Genetic Psychology Monographs*, 1970, *81*, 123–142.

Geisler, M. P., and Thrush, R. S. Counseling experiences and needs of older women students. *Journal of the NAWDAC*, 1975, *39*(1), 3–7.

Gelfand, D., Olsen, J. K., and Block, M. R. Two generations of elderly in the changing American family: implications for family services. *Family Coordinator*, 1978, *27*(4), 395–403.

Gerber, I. Anticipatory grief and aged widows and widowers. *Journal of Gerontology*, 1975, *30*(2), 225–229.

Gersuny, C. The rhetoric of the retirement home industry. *Gerontologist*, 1970, *10*(4, part I), 282–286.

Glenn, N. D. Psychological well-being in the postparental stage: some evidence from national surveys. *Journal of Marriage and the Family*, 1975, *37*(1), 105–110.

Glick, P. C. Perspectives on the living arrangements of the elderly. Paper presented at the 30th annual meeting of the Gerontological Society (San Francisco, Nov. 1977).

Green, D. E., and Nemzer, D. E. Changes in cigarette smoking by women: an analysis, 1966 and 1970. *Health Services Reports*, 1973, *88*(7), 631–636.

Hargreaves, A. G. Making the most of the middle years. *American Journal of Nursing*, 1975, *75*(10), 1772–1776.

Harris, J. *The Prime of Ms. America: The American Woman at Forty.* New York: Putnam, 1975.

Havighurst, R. J. The social competence of middle aged people. *Genetic Monographs,* 1957, *56,* 297–375.

Heyman, D. K., and Jeffers, F. C. Wives and retirement: a pilot study. *Journal of Gerontology,* 1968, *23,* 488–496.

———, and Gianturco, D. T. Long-term adaptation by the elderly to bereavement. *Journal of Gerontology,* 1973, *28,* 359–362.

Higgins, D. H. Female 'nestitis': self-concept, role flexibility, and achievement. Paper presented at the 28th annual meeting of the Gerontological Society (Louisville, Ky., Oct. 1975).

Hochschild, A. R. Communal life styles for the old. *Society,* 1973, *10*(5), 50–58.

Hoffman, H., and Wefring, L. R. Sex and age differences in psychiatric symptoms of alcoholics. *Psychological Reports,* 1972, *30*(3), 887–889.

Horrocks, J. E., and Mussman, M. C. Middlescence: age-related stress periods during adult years. *Genetic Psychology Monographs,* 1970, *82,* 119.

Hulicka, I. M., Morganti, B., and Cataldo, F. Perceived latitude of choice of institutionalized and non-institutionalized elderly women. *Experimental Aging Research,* 1975, *1*(1), 27–39.

Huyck, M. H. *Growing Older.* Englewood Cliffs: Prentice-Hall, 1974.

Hybels, J. H., and Mueller, M. W. Volunteer work: recognition and accreditation. In A. F. Cahn (ed.), *Women in Midlife—Security and Fulfillment (part 1).* Washington, D.C.: GPO, 1978.

Institute of Gerontology. *Minority Aging in America.* Ann Arbor: University of Michigan-Wayne State University, 1971.

Irey, N. S., and Froede, R. C. Evaluation of deaths from drug overdose, a clinicopathologic study. *American Journal of Clinical Pathology,* 1974, *61*(6), 778–784.

Jackson, H. Uncle Sam's aging black women. *Golden Page,* 1978, *2*(3), 16–20+.

Jackson, J. J. Comparative life styles and family and friend relationships among older black women. *Family Coordinator,* 1972a, *21*(4), 477–485.

———. Marital life among aging blacks. *Family Coordinator,* 1972b, *21*(1), 21–27.

———. Aged blacks: a potpourri in the direction of reduction of inequities. In J. J. Jackson (ed.), *Aging Black Women.* Philadelphia: National Caucus on the Black Aged, 1975.

———. Plights of older black women in the United States. *Black Aging,* 1975-76, *1*(2-3), 12–20.

Jacobs, R. H. A typology of older American women. *Social Policy,* 1976, *7*(3), 34–39.

Jacobson, D. Rejection of the retiree role: a study of female industrial workers in their 50's. *Human Relations,* 1974, *27*(5), 477–492.

Janeway, E. Breaking the age barrier. *Ms.,* 1973, *1*(10), 50–53+.

Johnson, M. Broadening elective and appointive political participation. In A. F.Cahn (ed.), *Women in Midlife—Security and Fulfillment (part 1)*. Washington, D.C.: GPO, 1978.

Jones, F. C. The lofty role of the black grandmother. *Crisis*, 1972, *80*(1). 19–21.

Jones, T. (ed.). Going strong in your eighties. *Quest*, 1978, *2*(2), 113–119.

Karcher, C. J., and Linden, L. L. Family rejection of the aged and nursing home utilization. *International Journal of Aging and Human Development*, 1974, *5*(3), 231–244.

Kastenbaum, R. Is death a life crisis? On the confrontation with death in theory and practice. In N. Datan and L. H. Ginsberg (eds.), *Life-Span Developmental Psychology: Normative Life Crises*. New York: Academic Press, 1975.

————, and Mishara, B. L. Premature death and self-injurious behavior in old age. *Geriatrics*, 1971, *26*(7), 71–81.

Katz, N. The subject as subject: a study of the returning woman student. *Council on Anthropology and Education Quarterly*, 1975, *6*(3), 19–22.

Kerckhoff, A. C. Family patterns and morale in retirement. In I. H. Simpson and J. C. McKinney (eds.), *Social Aspects of Aging*. Durham, N.C.: Duke University Press, 1966.

Kethley, A. J. Women and aging: the unforgivable sin. In J. R. Leppalauto (ed.), *Women on the Move*. Pittsburgh: Know, 1975.

Kimmel, D. C. *Adulthood and Aging*. New York: John Wiley, 1974.

Kinsey, A. C., Pomeroy, W. B., Martin, C. J., and Gebhard, O. H. *Sexual Behavior in the Human Female*. Philadelphia: W. B. Saunders, 1953.

Kline, C. The socialization process of women: implications for a theory of successful aging. *Gerontologist*, 1975, *15*(6), 486–492.

Kreps, J., and Clark, R. *Sex, Age, and Work: The Changing Composition of the Labor Force*. Baltimore: Johns Hopkins University Press, 1975.

Krupp, G. R., and Kligfeld, B. The bereavement reaction: a cross-cultural evaluation. *Journal of Religion and Health*, 1962, *1*(3), 222–246.

Kushner, R. *Breast Cancer: A Personal History and Investigative Report*. New York: Harcourt, Brace, Jovanovich, 1975.

Lambing, M. L. B. Social class living patterns of retired Negroes. *Gerontologist*, 1972, *12*(3), 285–288.

Larson, R. Thirty years of research on the subjective well-being of older Americans. *Journal of Gerontology*, 1978, *33*(1), 109–125.

Learoyd, B. M. Psychotropic drugs and the elderly patient. *Medical Journal of Australia*, 1972, *1*, 1131–1133.

Lemov, P. What you can't take with you. *Washingtonian*, 1977, (Oct.), 261–267.

Lenhart, D. G. The use of medications in the elderly population. *Nursing Clinics of North America*, 1976, *11*(1), 135–143.

Levi, L. *Stress: Sources, Management and Prevention; Medical and Psychological Aspects of the Stress of Everyday Life*. New York: Liveright, 1967.

Lewis, M. I., and Butler, R. N. Why is women's lib ignoring old women? *Aging and Human Development,* 1972, *3*(3), 223–231.

Lieberman, M. A. Psychological correlates of impending death: some preliminary observations. In B. Neugarten (ed.), *Middle Age and Aging.* Chicago: University of Chicago Press, 1968.

Lifshitz, K., and Kline, N. S. Psychopharmacology and the aged. *Journal of Gerontology,* 1961, *16,* 396.

Lindemann, E. Symptomatology and management of acute grief. *American Journal of Psychiatry,* 1944, *101*(2), 141–148.

Linn, L. S., and Davis, M. S. The use of psychotherapeutic drugs by middle-aged women. *Journal of Health and Social Behavior,* 1971, *12*(4), 331–340.

Lipman, A. Role conceptions and morale in couples in retirement. *Journal of Gerontology,* 1961, *16*(3), 267–271.

Livson, F. B. Patterns of personality development in middle-aged women: a longitudinal study. *International Journal of Aging and Human Development,* 1976, *7*(2), 107–115.

———. Cultural faces of Eve: images of women. Paper presented at annual meeting of the American Psychological Association (San Francisco, Aug. 1977).

Lopata, H. Z. The life cycle of the social role of the housewife. *Sociology and Social Research,* 1966, *51,* 5–22.

———. Social psychological aspects of role involvement. *Sociology and Social Research,* 1969, *53,* 285–299.

———. The social involvement of American widows. *American Behavioral Scientist,* 1970, *14*(1), 41–57.

———. *Widowhood in an American City.* Cambridge, Mass.: Schenkman, 1973.

———. Grief work and identity reconstruction. *Journal of Geriatric Psychiatry,* 1975a *8*(1), 41–55.

———. Social relationships of black and white widowed women in a northern metropolis. In J. J. Jackson (ed.), *Aging Black Women.* Philadelphia: National Caucus on the Black Aged, 1975b.

———. Widowhood: societal factors in life-span disruptions and alternatives. In N. Datan and L. H. Ginsberg (eds.), *Life-Span Developmental Psychology: Normative Life Crises.* New York: Academic Press, 1975c.

———. Changing roles: projections for the future and policy implications. In A. F. Cahn (ed.), *Women in Midlife—Security and Fulfillment (part 1).* Washington, D.C.: GPO, 1978.

———. *Women as Widows—Support Systems.* New York: Elsevier North Holland, 1979.

———, and Steinhart, F. Work histories of American urban women. *Gerontologist,* 1971, *11*(1, part II), 27–36.

Lowenthal, M. F. Psychosocial variations across the adult life course: frontiers for research and policy. *Gerontologist*, 1975, *15*(1, part I), 6–12.

———, Berkman, P., and Associates. *Aging and Mental Disorder in San Francisco*. San Francisco: Jossey-Bass, 1967.

———, and Haven, C. Interaction and adaptation: intimacy as a critical variable. *American Sociological Review*, 1968, *33*, 20–30.

———, Thurnher, M., and Chiriboga, D. *Four Stages of Life: A Comparative Study of Women and Men Facing Transition*. San Francisco: Jossey-Bass, 1975.

———, and Robinson, B. Social networks and isolation. In R. Binstock and E. Shanas (eds.), *Handbook of Aging and the Social Sciences*. New York: Van Nostrand Reinhold, 1976.

Lozier, J. Accommodating old people in society: examples from Appalachia and New Orleans. In N. Datan and L. H. Ginsberg (eds.), *Life-Span Developmental Psychology: Normative Life Crises*. New York: Academic Press, 1975.

Maas, S., and Kuypers, J. *From Thirty to Seventy: A Forty-year Longitudinal Study of Adult Life Styles and Personality*. San Francisco: Jossey-Bass, 1974.

Maletzky, B. M., and Klotter, J. Smoking and alcoholism. *American Journal of Psychiatry*, 1974, *131*(4), 445–447.

Martel, M. V. Age-sex roles in American magazine fiction (1890–1955). In B. Neugarten (ed.), *Middle Age and Aging*. Chicago: University of Chicago Press, 1968.

Masters, W. H., and Johnson, V. *Human Sexual Response*. Boston: Little, Brown, 1966.

McKain, W. *Retirement marriage*. Monograph No. 3. Storrs, Conn.: Storrs Agricultural Experiment Station, University of Connecticut, 1969.

———. A new look at old marriages. *Family Coordinator*, 1972, *21*, 60–61.

McKeithen, W. S. Major gynecological surgery in elderly females 65 years of age and older. *American Journal of Obstetrics and Gynecology*, 1975, *123*(1), 59–65.

Meals and Companionship for Senior Citizens. Washington, D.C.: Social and Rehabilitation Service, Administration on Aging, 1972.

Mintz, M. Pension system bias is argued in high court. *Washington Post*, Jan. 19, 1978, A-10.

Moore, J. W. Mexican-Americans. *Gerontologist*, 1971, *11*(1, part I), 30–35.

Morgan, L. A. A re-examination of widowhood and morale. *Journal of Gerontology*, 1976, *31*(6), 687–695.

Morgan, S. *Hysterectomy*. New York: Healthright, 1978.

Moss, Z. It hurts to be alive and obsolete: the aging woman. In R. Morgan (ed.), *Sisterhood is Powerful*. New York: Random House, 1970.

Mulvey, M. C. Psychological and sociological factors in prediction of career patterns of women. *Genetic Psychological Monographs*, 1973, No. 68.

Murphy, Y., and Murphy, R. F. Women and men. In P. C. Lee and R. S. Stewart (eds.), *Sex Differences: Cultural and Developmental Dimensions*. New York: Urizen Books, 1976.

Neugarten, B. L. *Personality in Middle and Late Life*. New York: Atherton Press, 1964.

———, and Gutman, D. L. Age-sex roles and personality in middle age: a thematic apperception study. In B. L. Neugarten (ed.), *Middle Age and Aging*. Chicago: University of Chicago Press, 1968.

———, and Weinstein, K. K. The changing American grandparent. In B. L. Neugarten (ed.), *Middle Age and Aging*. Chicago: University of Chicago Press, 1968.

———, Wood, V., Kraines, R. J., and Loomis, B. Women's attitudes toward the menopause. In B. L. Neugarten (ed.), *Middle Age and Aging*. Chicago: University of Chicago Press, 1968.

———, and Datan, N. Sociological perspectives on the life cycle. In P. Baltes and K. W. Schaie (eds.), *Life-Span Developmental Psychology: Personality and Socialization*. New York: Academic Press, 1973.

———. The middle years. In S. Arieti (ed.), *American Handbook of Psychiatry*, vol. 1. 2nd ed. New York: Basic Books, 1974.

———, and Brown-Rezanka, L. Midlife women in the 1980's. In A. F. Cahn (ed.), *Women in Midlife—Security and Fulfillment (part 1)*. Washington, D.C.: GPO, 1978.

Nielsen, M., Blenkner, M., Bloom, M., Downs, T., and Beggs, H. Older persons after hospitalization: a controlled home aide service. *American Journal of Public Health*, 1972, *62*(8), 1094–1101.

Northcott, H. C. Too young, too old—age in the world of television. *Gerontologist*, 1975, *15*(2), 184–186.

O'Brien, P. *Woman alone*. New York: Quadrangle, 1973.

Palmore, E. Differences in the retirement patterns of men and women. *The Gerontologist*, 1965, *5*(1), 4–8.

———. Attitudes toward aging as shown by humor. *Gerontologist*, 1971, *11*(3, part I), 181–186.

———. Total chance of institutionalization among the aged. *Gerontologist*, 1976, *16*(6), 504–407.

———, and Manton, K. Ageism compared to racism and sexism. *Journal of Gerontology*, 1973, *28*(3), 363–369.

Patterson, R. D., Abrahams, R., and Baker, F. Preventing self-destructive behavior. *Geriatrics*, 1974, *29*(11), 115–118, 121.

Paulshock, B. Z. What every woman should know about hysterectomy. *Today's Health*, 1976, *54*(2), 23–25.

Payne, B. P. Age differences in the meaning of leisure activities. Paper presented at the annual meeting of the Gerontological Society (Miami, 1973).

———, and Whittington, F. Older women—examination of popular stereotypes and research evidence. *Social Problems*, 1976, *23*(4), 488–504.

Pearlin, L. I. Sex roles and depression. In N. Datan and L. H. Ginsberg (eds.), *Life-Span Developmental Psychology: Normative Life Crises*. New York: Academic Press, 1975.

Pelletier, K. R. *Mind as Healer, Mind as Slayer*. New York: Dell, 1977.

Perry, P. W. The night of ageism. In H. Cox (ed.), *Focus: Aging*. Guilford, Conn.: Dushkin Publishing Group, 1978.

Petersen, D. M., and Thomas, C. W. Acute drug reactions among the elderly. *Journal of Gerontology*, 1975, *30*(5), 552–556.

Peterson, B. Life in a microcosm has a bittersweet flavor. *Washington Post*, May 14, 1979, A-1.

Pfeiffer, E. Survival in old age: physical, psychological, and social correlates of longevity. *Journal of the American Geriatrics Society*, 1970, *20*, 151–157.

Pihlblad, C. T. and Adams, D. L. Widowhood, social participation and life satisfaction. *International Journal of Aging and Human Development*, 1972, 3(4), 323–330.

Pineo, P. C. Disenchantment in the later years of marriage. In M. Sussman (ed.), *Sourcebook in Marriage and the Family*. New York: Houghton Mifflin, 1968.

Pishkin, V., and Thorne, F. C. A factorial structure of the dimensions of femininity in alcoholic, schizophrenic, and normal populations. *Journal of Clinical Psychology*, 1977, *33*(1), 10–17.

Posner, J. It's all in your head: feminist and medical models of menopause (strange bedfellows). *Sex Roles*, 1979, *5*(2), 179–190.

Powell, B. The empty nest, employment, and psychiatric symptoms in college-educated women. *Psychology of Women Quarterly*, 1977, *2*, 35–43.

Powers, E. A., and Bultena, G. L. Sex differences in intimate friendships in old age. *Journal of Marriage and the Family*, 1976, *38*(4), 739–747.

Prock, V. N. The middle years: the mid-stage woman. *American Journal of Nursing*, 1975, *75*(6), 1019–1021.

Ragan, P. K. Socialization for the retirement role: cooling the mark out. Paper presented at the annual meeting of the American Psychological Association (San Francisco, Aug. 1977).

Releasing the potential of the older volunteer. Los Angeles: Ethel Percy Andrus Gerontology Center, 1976.

Renne, K. Correlates of dissatisfaction in marriage. *Journal of Marriage and the Family*, 1970, *32*, 54–67.

Resnik, H., and Cantor, J. M. Suicide and aging. *Journal of the American Geriatric Society*, 1970, *18*, 152–158.

Rich, S. Enrollment hits new low for the '70s. *Washington Post,* May 15, 1979, A.

Riley, M., and Foner, A. *Aging and Society, Vol I, An Inventory of Research Findings.* New York: Russell Sage Foundation, 1968.

Rollins, B. C., and Cannon, K. Marital satisfaction over the life cycle: a reevaluation. *Journal of Marriage and the Family,* 1974, *36,* 271–282.

Rooney, R. Middle age divorce—the family time bomb. *Parade (Washington Post),* Mar. 5, 1978. 6–7.

Rosow, I. Housing and local ties of the aged. In B. L. Neugarten (ed.), *Middle Age and Aging.* Chicago: University of Chicago Press, 1968.

Safilios-Rothschild, C. Sexuality, power, and freedom among "older" women. In L. Troll, J. Israel, and K. Israel (eds.), *Looking Ahead.* Englewood Cliffs: Prentice-Hall, 1977.

Sarton, M. Toward another dimension. *Women,* 1976, *4*(4), 26–27.

Saul, S. *Aging: An Album of People Growing Old.* New York: John Wiley, 1974.

Seguin, M. M. Opportunity for peer socialization in a retirement community. *Gerontologist,* 1973, *13*(2), 208–214.

Sheehy, G. *Passages: Predictable Crises of Adult Life.* New York: E. P. Dutton, 1976.

Siegel, J. S. Demographic aspects of aging and the older population in the United States. *Current Population Reports.* Series P-23, No. 59. Washington, D.C.: GPO, 1976.

Silverman, P. Widowhood and preventive intervention. *Family Coordinator,* 1972, *21,* 95–102.

———, and Cooperband, A. Mutual help and the elderly widow. *Journal of Geriatric Psychiatry,* 1975, *8*(1), 9–27.

Simos, B. G. Relations of adults with aging parents. *Gerontologist,* 1970, *10,* 135–139.

Smith, B. K. *Aging in America.* Boston: Beacon, 1973.

Sokolowska, M. Some reflections on the different attitudes of men and women toward work. *International Labor Review,* 1965, *92*(1), 35–50.

Sommers, T., and Shields, L. Problems of the displaced homemaker. In A. F. Cahn (ed.), *Women in Midlife—Security and Fulfillment (part I).* Washington, D.C.: GPO, 1978.

Sontag, S. The double standard of aging. *Saturday Review,* 1972, *55*(38), 29–38.

Sowell, T. Ethnicity in a changing America. *Daedalus,* 1978, *107,* 213.

Spanier, G., Lewis, R., and Cole, C. Marital adjustment over the life cycle: the issue of curvilnearity. *Journal of Marriage and the Family,* 1975, *37,* 263–275.

Spence, D., and Lonner, T. The "empty nest": a transition within motherhood. *Family Coordinator,* 1971, *20*(4), 369–376.

Strax, P. *Early detection.* New York: Harper and Row, 1974.

Streib, G. F. Older families and their troubles: familial and social responses. *The Family Coordinator*, 1972, *21*(1), 5–19.

———. Social stratification and aging. In R. H. Binstock and E. Shanas (eds.), *Handbook of Aging and the Social Sciences*. New York: Van Nostrand Reinhold, 1976.

———, and Haug, M. Alternative housing arrangements. In A. F. Cahn (ed.), *Women in Midlife—Security and Fulfillment (part I)*. Washington, D.C.: GPO, 1978.

———, and Schneider, C. J. *Retirement in American Society: Impact and Process*. Ithaca: Cornell University Press, 1971.

Stub, H. R. Family structure and the social consequences of death. In J. R. Folta and E. S. Deck (eds.), *A Sociological Framework for Patient Care*. New York: John Wiley, 1966.

Swenson, W. M. Attitudes toward death in an aged population. *Journal of Gerontology*, 1961, *16*(1), 49–52.

Taietz, P. Two conceptual models of the senior center. *Journal of Gerontology*, 1976, *31*(2), 219–222.

Taines, B. Older women, newer students. *Community and Junior College Journal*, 1973, *44*(1), 17.

Task Force on Older Women. *Quarterly Newsletter*, 1975, 2(2).

Tonna, E. A. Aging of skeletal-dental systems and supporting tissues. In C. E. Finch and L. Hayflick (eds.), *Handbook of the Biology of Aging*. New York: Van Nostrand Reinhold, 1977.

Troll, L. The family of later life: a decade review. *Journal of Marriage and the Family*, 1971, 33(2), 263–290.

———, and Turner, J. Overcoming age-sex discrimination. In A. F. Cahn (ed.), *Women in Midlife—Security and Fulfillment (part I)*. Washington, D.C.: GPO, 1978.

U.S. Department of Commerce, Bureau of the Census. A statistical portrait of women in the U.S. *Current Population Reports*, Series P-23, No. 58. Washington, D.C.: GPO, 1976a.

———. Special studies: demographic aspects of aging and the older population. *Current Population Reports*, Series P-23, No. 59. Washington, D.C.: GPO, 1976b.

———. Projections of the population of the United States: 1977 to 2050. *Current Population Reports*, Series P-25, No. 704. Washington, D.C.: GPO, 1977a.

———. *Social Indicators 1976*. Washington, D.C.: GPO, 1977b. U.S. Department of Health, Education and Welfare (DHEW), Administration on Aging. Elderly widows. *Statistical Memo No. 33*. Washington, D.C.: GPO, 1976.

————. American Indian population 55 years of age and older: geographic distribution, 1970. *Statistical Reports on Older Americans*. Washington, D.C.: GPO, 1977.

U.S. Department of Labor. *1975 Handbook on Women Workers*. Bulletin No. 297. Washington, D.C.: GPO, 1975.

————. Women's Bureau. *Women with Low Incomes*. Washington, D.C.: GPO, 1977.

Walker, A. In search of our mothers' gardens. *Southern Exposure*, 1977, 4(4), 60–64.

Walsh, R. P. and Connor, C. L. *Old Men and Young Women: Partners in Discrimination*. Los Angeles: Loyola Marymount University, 1977.

Warren, H. H. Self-perception of independence among urban elderly. *American Journal of Occupational Therapy*, 1974, 28(6), 329–336.

Watress, W. It's something inside you. *Southern Exposure*, 1977, 4(4), 76–81.

Wax, J. It's like your own home here. *New York Times Magazine*, Nov. 21, 1976, 38–40, 87–102.

Weiss, J. Suicide in the aged. In H. L. P. Resnik (ed.), *Suicidal Behaviors: Diagnosis and Management*. Boston: Little, Brown, 1968.

Weissman, M. M. The depressed woman: recent research. *Social Work*, 1972, 17(5), 19–25.

Women's Medical Center. *Menopause*. Washington, D.C.: Women's Medical Center, 1977.

Wood, V., and Robertson, J. F. The satisfaction of grandparenthood. In J. F. Gubrium (ed.), *Time, Roles, and Self in Old Age*. New York: Behavioral Publications, 1976.

Wynne, R. D., and Heller, F. Drug overuse among the elderly: a growing problem. *Perspective on Aging*, 1973, *11*, 1518.

Young, F., and Young, L. *Everything You Should Know About Pension Plans*. Bethesda, Md.: Bethesda Books, 1976.

Zanar, E. Reentry ripoff. *Ms.*, 1977, 6(5), 83–86+.

Zimmerman, D. R. Medicine today: breast cancer. *Ladies Home Journal*, 1974, (June), 22.

■ Index

Index